Wisdom from Women in the Bible

Edith Deen

Wisdom
from
Women
in the
Bible

Published in San Francisco by
HARPER & ROW, PUBLISHERS
New York, Hagerstown, San Francisco, London

Bible Sources:

Harper's Bible Dictionary, Madeleine S. and J. Lane Miller, Harper and Brothers, 1956.

The New English Bible, Books of Wisdom and Ecclesiasticus in *The Apocrypha,* Oxford University Press, Cambridge University Press, 1970.

King James Version The Holy Bible, (referred to as KJV), Harper and Brothers, Publishers.

Revised Standard Version, with introductions, annotations, topical headings, marginal references, and index, prepared and edited by Harold Lindsell, Harper and Row, 1964. This is the basic text for this book unless otherwise indicated.

The Moffat Bible, James Moffat, Harper and Brothers, New York and London, 1954.

Other Sources:

de Balzac, *To Mother with Love,* Frederick Ungar, editor, Stephen Daye Press, 1951, Pgs. 335-337.

Crook, Margaret Brackenbury, *Women and Religion*, Beacon Press, Boston, 1964, pg. 249-251.

Deen, *All of the Women of the Bible,* Harper and Row, 1955, Great Women of the Christian Faith, Harper and Row, 1959. Prayer of Queen Isabella of Castile (1451-1504) pg. 71.

"The Least Coin" by Sara Lindsay from *In Quest of the Least Coin* by Grace Nies Fletcher. Copyright © 1968 by Grace Nies Fletcher. By permission of William Morrow & Company

Gibran, Kahlil, *The Prophet,* Alfred A. Knopf, 1971, On Giving Chapters 45 and 49.

Morrison, James Dalton, *Masterpieces of Religious Verse,* Harper and Brothers, 1948. These eight poems below are from this collection.

FIRST EDITION

Designed by Leigh McLellan

Library of Congress Cataloging in Publication Data

Deen, Edith.
    Wisdom from women in the Bible.

        1. Women in the Bible. I. Title.
BS575.D43   1978   248'.843   77-20460
ISBN 0-06-061851-5

78 79 80 81 82   10   9   8   7   6   5   4   3   2   1

Contents

Preface

Wisdom from Women in the Bible is based upon the actual dialogues and experiences of women who lived more than two thousand years ago. It completes a trilogy about women in the Bible and shows that advice, first given long ago, can be passed on from one generation to another.

The first book in this trilogy, *All of the Women of the Bible,* is biographical. The second, *The Bible's Legacy for Womanhood,* highlights precepts regarding womanhood as a whole. This, the third, deals with marriage, home, possessions, children, and widowhood and with the spirtual awareness that can come through believing in an ever-listening, ever-loving God.

God has never been more radiant in my life than during these last three years as I have studied the wisdom, hopes, dreams, and ambitions of these women. I have also included the follies of some of them, for life, both then and now, is a learning process; we gain as much from our mistakes as from our victories.

I know better now that wisdom is a quality finer than jewels and with a yield greater than gold. I perceive more clearly that a daily walk with God produces wisdom, a walk away from God produces only folly.

For the first time, I have turned occasionally to the apocryphal books the Wisdom of Solomon and Ecclesiasticus (or the Wisdom of Jesus son of Sirach). But the major part of my emphasis comes from Proverbs, the greatest book on wisdom in literature. I have also found an endless amount of material in other parts of the Old and New Testaments.

I have been constantly amazed and inspired. After twenty-five years of writing about the Bible, I have learned that its meaning is constantly renewing itself in the mind of the reader and revealing broad avenues of thought to the seeker after truth.

The idea for this book flashed like a light across my path one Sunday morning as I walked up the ramp of my own church,

University Christian in Fort Worth, Texas, my church home for forty years. If women from Genesis to the present learn from God's timeless message, I thought, why not write the last of the trilogy, proclaiming the sameness of all women's problems, both in primitive days and now? In other words, the Bible is an expanding, pragmatic book, educational, poetic, inspiring, at once original and eternal.

However, it was with hesitation that I mentioned this concept to my editor, Marie Cantlon, whom I had first known as a young girl at Harper & Row when I started my first book. Fortunately, she liked the new idea. But I soon found out it was no small task to evolve a readable, workable book based on ancient women that filled a need for the woman today.

This book, like five others, has been written in a serene home in an old setting, and with the same helpers. First, I wish to thank my neighbor, Ella Higginbotham, who has typed the manuscript when she really did not have the time and who managed to produce legible copy out of my heavily edited notes.

I also want to express gratitude to my capable housekeeper, Versie Roberts, who has set me free from home duties in order that I might spend long hours in my study.

Another friend, Grace Nies Fletcher, a newcomer from New England to my home city, has made invaluable suggestions. As the author of sixteen books herself, a teacher of creative writing in three universities, and a member of the advisory board of the Christian Herald Bookshelf for more than two decades, I have had confidence in her wise counsel.

So I send this book forth with the hope that it will inspire a deeper study of the Bible and that it will help others gain a new wisdom and understanding in handling their daily problems. This is one of the wonders of the Bible. Any theme one chooses turns out to be contemporary.

In writing this book I have learned what a joy it is to lose consciousness of self in a task one loves. I am indeed a free woman. What more could one ask?

Section I
In the Beginning

"Wisdom is a breath of the power of God,
a pure emanation of the glory of the Almighty
a reflection of the eternal light
a spotless mirror of the working of God
and an image of his goodness" (paraphrase from the Wis. of Sol.
7:25-27, NEB).

In the first books of the Bible wisdom revolves around a search for the meaning of life. Other early books in the Old Testament continue to unfold God's goodness in the lives of his people. In their search for God during seemingly impossible situations, the early women of the Bible came to know the power of a God of infinite wisdom. They were sure that "the wise, and their works, are in the hand of God" (Ecclesiastes 9:1, KJV).

Chapter 1

From Tribulation to Joy:
Eve

(Gen. 4:1–26)

"God has given me another child instead of Abel, whom Cain killed," said Eve, the wife of Adam, when their last named son Seth was born. Eve's tribulation, the narrative implies, was her testing time. Amid her grief over the loss of her most promising son, Abel, and the blighted hope in her wayward son, Cain, she must have suffered poignant heartaches.

It is easy to believe that Eve, like all mothers during periods of family tragedy, learned to turn to God for comfort. He was her fortress and strength, or she could not have spoken so joyfully when Seth was born. Her buoyant reaction suggests that after Seth's birth she gained a new perspective and that she was to know, as Job later learned, that God is just and that he does not fail those who serve and patiently wait on him.

A sorrowing mother like Eve was sure to learn also that God never lets us grieve for long. He teaches us to walk upon the high places, where we come to a better understanding of the psalmist's words:

"God is our refuge and strength,
    a very present help in trouble.
Therefore we will not fear though the earth should change,
    though the mountains shake in the heart of the seas;
        though its waters roar and foam,
    though the mountains tremble with its tumult" (Ps. 46:1–3).

Eve's family is typical of the human family at its worst and at its best. All of us, like Eve, dwell in and out of the Lord's presence. Eve first left God's presence when the serpent (evil) tempted her to eat of the forbidden fruit and when she influenced Adam to do the same.

The life pattern of Eve and her family, though briefly described in the Bible, follows the cycle of family living. Eve is first depicted as young and beautiful, dwelling in a lush garden where she had begun her life. Then after yielding to temptation, she is seen amid the tragedies of motherhood. She no doubt sought God in order to surmount her sorrow after her farewell to Cain, a murderer who went out from the presence of the Lord.

The latter part of Eve's story, call it a legend if you will, reminds us of Jesus' farewell address to his disciples: "So you have sorrow now, but I will see you again and your hearts will rejoice, and no one will take your joy from you" (John 16:22).

What a blessed promise this is for all of us. It can be especially comforting to a mother, who like Eve, mourns both the evils and the sorrows of her family.

In her affliction Eve was typical of mothers as a whole. Although sorely grieved over the evil in Cain, she learned, just as we must learn, to draw nearer to God, who loves us and who opens new doors when others close.

Eve's new door opened upon Seth, who was followed by a godly generation. That we know, for "at that time men began to call upon the name of the Lord" (Gen. 4:26), and Eve was filled with joy once again. Her tragedies and subsequent spiritual renewal assure us that the Lord will deliver us from the heartaches of tragedy and sorrow if we diligently seek him and then strive to do his will. All the wise Eves of today will find inspiration in these words from a 19th Century hymn set to the music of a Brahms Chorals:

> Let nothing ever grieve thee, distress thee, nor fret thee;
> Heed God's good will, my soul, be still, compose thee.
> Why brood all day in sorrow? Tomorrow will bring thee God's
> help benign,
> And grace sublime in mercy.
> Be true in all endeavors and ever ply bravely, what God decrees
> brings joy and peace, He'll stay thee.

We can infer that Eve, a woman brought forth in God's image, had the wisdom to know that God created her womanly being, that through him she learned the wonder of parenthood, and that God ordained for her life an unending pattern of spiritual truths. She was far-sighted enough to draw nearer to God in all of his wonder. Toward the end of her life, as she gained in strength and understanding, she also grew in wisdom and love for God her creator.

> "Wisdom was first of all created things;
> intelligent purpose has been there from the beginning"
> Ecclesiasticus 1:4–5, NEB.

Chapter 2

A Wife with Love and Status:
Sarah

(Gen. 12, 6–18, 20–21)

No woman in ancient times was freer than Sarah, the wife of Abraham, the first patriarch. Through Abraham, who treated her as equal, she became the mother of Isaac (the son of promise) and the grandmother of Esau and Jacob. Through Jacob, Sarah was the great-grandmother of the heads of the twelve tribes of Israel.

Outspoken, completely uninhibited, independent, and wise, Sarah handed down a rich heritage to her family as its first and most honored matriarch.

Wherever Abraham went, he proudly consigned the first place to Sarah. She rode beside him as copartner in their long caravan composed of servants as well as sheep, oxen, asses, herds, flocks, and supplies. Together Abraham and Sarah trekked from Haran around the Fertile Crescent to the trail south along the Mediterranean, along the level banks of the Euphrates, through the rich valley of the Nile, and finally into the land of Canaan.

Not as chattel but as a wife, Sarah was with her husband when he went to the court of Abimilech in Gerar. Because she was beautiful, the king wanted to take Sarah into his harem, and he did for a short time; but Sarah's fidelity to Abraham and his faith in her secured her escape. She was miraculously released by Abimilech, and together she and Abraham journeyed back to Canaan.

For many years Sarah lacked freedom in only one area of her

life. She was barren and despaired of ever giving birth to a child. Finally she said to Abraham, "The Lord has prevented me from bearing children; go in to my maid; it may be that I shall obtain children by her" (Gen. 16:2). And Abraham went in unto Hagar, Sarah's Egyptian maid.

Sarah became a prisoner in her own home, for the maid became proud and arrogant toward Sarah, her mistress. The troubled Sarah said to Abraham, "May the wrong done to me be on you! I gave my maid to your embrace, and when she saw that she had conceived, she looked on me with contempt. May the Lord judge between you and me!" (Gen. 16:5).

Still recognizing Sarah's rights as a wife, Abraham said to her, "Your maid is in your power; do to her as you please." Sarah dealt harshly with Hagar, and Hagar fled; but at an angel's insistence she returned and gave birth to her son Ishmael. Later when Sarah, in her old age, miraculously gave birth to Isaac, Hagar became more insolent than ever to her mistress. Like his mother, Ishmael scoffed at Sarah's son. (However, Ishmael in later years took his place as the revered ancestor of the Arabs through his father Abraham). (This family division is still a matter of Hebrew-Arab struggle.)

Sarah took her stand against Ishmael and his mother Hagar in a manner that may be better understood by a phrase in Prov. 30:21, 23, which states that "Under three things the earth trembles." One of these is when a maid succeeds her mistress in her wifely rights. It is natural then than Sarah, human as she was, should say to Abraham, "Cast out this slave woman with her son; for the son of this slave woman shall not be heir with my son Isaac" (Gen. 21:10).

Abraham listened to his wife of many years, whom he still loved devotedly. He recognized that God created man and woman in his image and that they were therefore equal; so he sent Hagar and Ishmael away, and they went into the desert never to return.

This incident was not to Sarah's credit, but she is never without honor. Centuries later, it was written:

> "Look to the rock from which you were hewn,
>   and to the quarry from which you were digged.
> Look to Abraham your father
>   and to Sarah who bore you" (Isa. 51:1-2).

Despite her faults, Sarah was a rock in her character, one that came from a deep quarry.

Galatians states that Abraham had two sons, one by a slave and one by a free woman: "But the son of the slave was born according to the flesh, the son of the free woman through promise" (Gal. 4:23).

Sarah's son was born after she was old. Paul tells us that this was possible only through faith; so in this sense Sarah was a mother of faith.

Sarah was one of the wisest women among ancient Hebrews. She saved her marriage. She gave her son Isaac his rightful birthright. She protected her home from destruction by another woman and at the same time retained the love of her husband.

She never ran away from difficult situations or allowed her feet to stumble along the way. With fortitude and courage, she faced whatever came, and so she lives on as the esteemed wife of the first patriarch of the ancient Hebrews, who honor her to this day.

Like Sarah, wise men and women protect their homes and marriages; the foolish ones tear theirs down with their own hands.

The husband or wife who forfeits spiritual aspirations and claims what is sometimes called freedom may learn too late that he or she has lost everything else—the love and respect of spouse, children, and friends. He or she may discover himself or herself still in bondage, in some respects greater bondage than before. Real freedom involves more than selfish human rights, important as they are.

As Sarah's example shows, these human rights do not come easily. They come through sacrificing one's self and through suffering and strictly adhering to what is right and good. When one learns to conduct oneself with the kind of faith and love that generate in others wonder and warmth and a belief in God, one is as free as any human being can become.

Chapter 3

No Time for Angels:
Lot's Wife

(Gen. 19:1–38; Luke 17:32)

Lot's wife was so bound up in the worldly pleasures of Sodom and Gomorrah that she could not forsake them. Even after angels in the guise of men offered her the opportunity to escape to a little village in the mountains with her husband and her daughters, she lingered. The sun was shining as Lot and his daughters safely reached the village, but Lot's wife looked back and "became a pillar of salt."

Lot's wife was a niece by marriage of Abraham, the man of faith. When God informed Abraham that Sodom and Gomorrah would be destroyed because of their sins, Abraham interceded, asking God, "Will you destroy the righteous with the wicked?"

"Suppose there are fifty righteous left within the city?" he asked. God answered that he would save the city if there were fifty righteous. Abraham then asked if God would spare the city if there were forty-five or forty or thirty or twenty or ten righteous ones. Apparently there were not even ten.

It seems evident from the Bible discourse that Lot's wife was one of the wicked ones as were her sons-in-law; but not even the company of her husband and daughters fleeing to safety could lure her away. Even after she saw the smoke rising up like a burning furnace into a foreboding sky, she could not move forward. She refused even after she remembered that the night before the men of the city, young and old, had surrounded her house to commit sodomy with two angels in the guise of men who were their guests. Even after the Sodomites threatened to knock Lot's door down and to deal harshly with him as well as his guests, she stayed.

Little is recorded about Lot's wife. Could her life have been so frivolous that there was nothing about her worthy of mention? Perhaps her conversation ran something like this:

"Lot, let's build a stone house facing Sodom and Gomorrah. Our tent on the outskirts is not imposing enough."

Or, "Lot, the towers of Sodom and Gomorrah blaze in the distance, beckoning us to be part of the night life there. I long to be there even now as I look out upon our fertile plains of the Jordan, the ones your Uncle Abraham gave you the right to choose. And remember you took the best."

She might then have added, "I'm glad you chose this location. Our daughters might not have married men from such gay places as Sodom and Gomorrah."

What a travesty in words! Lot's wife never was able to see how little her worldly ambitions meant. Even as she left her home, she did not realize the insecure pillars upon which it had rested.

The few words about Lot's wife, "she became a pillar of salt," reveal how she reacted in a family crisis. Had she gone all the way with her husband and daughters and not turned back before they reached the village in the mountains, she might have averted the later wickedness of her family—the drunkenness of her husband and the incestuous behavior of her daughters toward their father.

Jesus teaches us much about Lot's wife in his profound discourse on how people went about their daily business—eating and drinking, buying and selling, planting and building—until the morning Lot left Sodom. Then fire and brimstone rained down from heaven, destroying all that were there. Jesus compared this day of destruction to the day "when the Son of man is revealed." "Remember Lot's wife," he admonished his listeners. "Whoever seeks to gain his life will lose it, but whoever loses his life will preserve it" (Luke 17:32-33).

In her longing to go back to her old life, Lot's wife lost not only all her material possessions but life itself. As she looked back, geologists explain, she died beneath an encrustment of salt that was caused by an explosion of the rock salt that lies beneath the mountains of Sodom on the west shore of the Dead sea (*All of the Women of the Bible*, p. 20). What a tragedy when angel hands could have led her to safety and salvation.

Every age produces prototypes of Lot's wife. More concerned with the quantity and quality of what they have than with the gift of life, they drink too much, spend money foolishly, and attempt to satisfy any passing desire. Immorality becomes a fashionable way of life they have no wish to abandon.

Only in the context of Jesus' discourse on Lot's wife can we begin to see how easy it is to depart from his example that glorifies sacrifice and suffering for others and in which the kingdom of God is not far away but in the midst of those who seek him.

Lot's wife typifies an ancient woman who had neither wisdom nor understanding. In one of his allegories, Ezekiel depicted the unwise daughters of Sodom who, like Lot's wife, had too much pride, too much food and ease, and were "haughty and did abominable things" (Eze. 16:50). Homes and families suffer when parents live with thought for themselves uppermost. In her indiscretion Lot's wife reminds us that,

> "Wisdom builds her house,
> but folly with her own hands tears it down. . . .
> The house of the wicked will be destroyed,
> but the tent of the upright will flourish" (Prov. 14:1, 11).

Chapter 4

Human Frailty:
Rebekah

(Gen. 24, 27, 28)

"Upon me be your curse, my son; only obey my word" (Gen. 27:13), spoke Rebekah to Jacob as she schemed to get him the family blessing that was the birthright of her son Esau, Jacob's twin. Had her husband, Isaac, not been blind, he might have seen that the aging Rebekah had slowly changed. She bore no resemblance to the helpful, compassionate Rebekah who had once said to Abraham's steward when he came seeking a bride for Abraham's son Isaac, "I will draw for your camels also, until they are no longer thirsty." She quickly emptied her jar into the trough and ran again to the well to draw enough water for all his camels.

Abraham's steward gazed at her in silence to learn if the Lord had prospered his journey from Canaan to the city of Nahor in Mesopotamia. Now he knew that the beautiful, courteous, thoughtful Rebekah was the right bride for his master's son. What's more she was the daughter of Abraham's nephew.

When she was asked if she would go into a new country and become the wife of his master's son Isaac, without hesitation she answered, "I will go." She was a woman of decision and adventure.

As she and her maids arrived in the Negeb, accompanied by Abraham's steward, she lifted up her eyes and asked, "Who is the man yonder, walking in the field to meet us?" The servant answered, "He is my master." Then Isaac took her into the tent, and she became his wife. He loved her and she comforted him after the death of his mother, Sarah.

Nothing but joy and kindness seemed to surround the young Rebekah. She and her husband were married twenty years when their twin sons were born, Esau first, and then Jacob. Then troubles set in. Esau was careless and was a glutton for food. Rebekah was never satisfied with the women he chose. One of her last recorded remarks was "I am sick and tired of Esau's Hittite women. If Jacob marries one, what good will my life be to me?" By this time Esau had taken a second wife from the Hittites, a pagan people.

But Jacob married the beautiful Rachel, whom he loved at first sight and through all the years of his life. If only Rebekah, instead of scheming, had been patient a little longer. But like all of us, Rebekah had her human frailties, and one was her ambitious plans for her favorite son Jacob. Nothing else mattered—not the good will of her aging, blind husband or the respect of her son Esau. Rebekah achieved her purpose by deceiving both of them. She won her desire, but she lost Jacob, who was forced to flee home and did not return until twenty years later, after his mother had died.

These were Rebekah's words to Jacob: "Now therefore, my son, obey my voice; arise, flee to Laban my brother in Haran, and stay with him awhile, until your brother's fury turns away; . . . and he forgets what you have done to him; then I will send, and fetch you from there. Why should I be bereft of you both in one day?" (Gen. 27:43-45).

Had Rebekah prayed for wisdom, God would have shown her another way to achieve his purpose. Wisdom was born with creation, but it took men and women centuries to learn its secrets, to fathom its meaning, and to discover that wisdom and understanding walk side by side. Rebekah had not learned the kind of wisdom spoken of in Proverbs:

"The Lord gives wisdom
from his mouth come knowledge and understanding;
he stores up sound wisdom for the upright;
he is a shield to those who walk in integrity, . . .
for wisdom will come into your heart,
and knowledge will be pleasant to your soul;
discretion will watch over you;
understanding will guard you;
delivering you from the way of evil" (Prov. 2:6-7, 10-12).

Rebekah did not wait for God to show her the right way to go, nor did she walk in integrity. Wisdom did not guard her, and she walked right into a disillusioning situation all by herself.

But she learned that God does not punish us for all our human frailties. Time heals many of them. Little did Rebekah dream that Jacob, for whom she had such great dreams, would achieve a more distinguished place in history than she had planned. How could she have known that he would become the direct ancestor of the Hebrew nation, be given the new name of Israel, and be the father of the twelve tribes of Israel?

Nor did she ever dream that the beautiful Rachel, far superior to Esau's wives, would become Jacob's most beloved wife. She never saw Rachel, and she never knew that one day there would be a grandson like the noble Joseph, Rachel's first son.

Rebekah lost her relationship with God for a time, but her son found God at Bethel, on his way to Haran. At Bethel he had a dream in which God promised to keep him wherever he went and bring him back to his homeland. Twenty years later he did.

Jacob never forgot that it was on his journey from home that he had stumbled into a new way of life, into a new home he called "the awesome entrance to heaven."

Many of us, like Rebekah, force our way out of a predicament instead of trusting God to solve it in his own way. Whether we realize it or not, God works in a mysterious way, his wonders to perform. Patient waiting is often all that God requires of us.

Chapter 5

The Miracle of Love:
Rachel

(Gen. 29, 30, 35)

Childbearing was the chief function of patriarchal wives. In ancient times a woman who failed to bear a child during the early years of her marriage became depressed, frustrated, irritable. Jacob's beloved wife Rachel was defeated at her inability to bear children and was sure she would go through life without them.

"Give me children, or I shall die" (Gen. 30:1), she complained to Jacob, who loved her devotedly, much more than he did her sister Leah, his other wife.

Rachel loved Jacob as much as he loved her but was finally so discouraged at her infertility that she told him, "Here is my maid Bilhah; go in to her, that she may bear upon my knees, and even I may have children through her" (Gen. 30:3). Jacob lay with Bilhah, who conceived and bore him a son. Rachel then said, "God has judged me, has also heard my voice and given me a son." Later Bilhah bore Jacob a second son.

Rachel's sister Leah, who already had two sons of her own, now presented her maid Zilpah to Jacob as a concubine. She gave birth to Jacob's next two sons, making eight in all. Leah later also had two other sons by Jacob.

Finally, however, Rachel bore Jacob a son of their own, Joseph, who was the joy of his life, even into his old age. "God has taken away my reproach," Rachel sighed. Then she asked, "May the Lord add to me another son!" Later after the family left Haran and returned to Canaan, Rachel's request was granted. When they were a short distance from Ephrath (Bethelem), Benjamin was born. (Jacob now had twelve sons, who became heads of the twelve tribes of Israel.)

While Rachel was giving birth to Benjamin, the midwives said to her, "Fear not; for now you will have another son." But Rachel died at the birth of this son and was buried near Bethehem. There Jacob set a monument of stones upon her grave, which survives to this day. Because of all her heartaches before the birth of her two sons, Rachel wanted to call the second Benoni ("son of my sorrow"), but Jacob named him Benjamin ("son of the right hand").

No matter how Rachel must have felt about her long wait for sons, she had been blessed with Jacob's love since the first day they met; and he never forgot the loss of his beautiful and beloved Rachel. Years later when he blessed his grandsons, Ephraim and Manasseh, the sons of Joseph, he kissed and embraced them, remembering full well that they were the heirs of his beautiful Rachel.

There is a great gulf between Rachel's world and that of the young woman's today, between Jacob's need for sons in primitive times and the independence of the young man today. Jacob's twelve sons, by two wives and two concubines, strengthened and protected his land and all he had. They were his sheepherders, his tillers of the soil, his merchandisers, and his strength in old age. In those times children were referred to as "the fruit of the womb" and "the heritage of the Lord."

Mores and customs have changed since the time of Rachel. The population rate has accelerated; so have the costs of rearing and educating children. It is natural that today young men and women ask themselves, "How can we meet the demands of a large family?"

Because of these and other pressures, abortions have become more common, and the issue is today the focus of raging controversy. Unlike Rachel, who was irritable because she could not have children, some young mothers today are irritable because they do not want the responsibility of children. They are jealous, not of women with children, but of women with successful careers, who seem to be much freer than they are. Today some women, and some men, are sacrificing the love and goodwill of their mate in order to put a career first. The wrong decision at this period can seriously damage a person's life. Like Rachel, he or she may bear a grudge against God, but for a different reason. In desperation some join false cults and other off-beat movements, most of them completely out of God's realm.

Children born into homes of love and order are still a great joy and humankind's hope of immortality. It is no small wonder that abortion has become such an explosive subject. No matter in what century or where we live, we cannot lose our desire for little children, children filled with a sense of wonder, children who will bring forth the miracles of tomorrow, children who teach us more than we can ever teach them.

Jesus said, "Truly, I say to you, unless you turn and become like children, you will not enter the kingdom of heaven. Whoever humbles himself like this child, he is greatest in the kingdom of heaven. Whoever receives one such child in my name receives me; but whoever causes one of these little ones who believe in me to sin, it would be better for him to have a great millstone fastened round his neck and to be drowned in the depth of the sea" (Matt. 18:3-6).

Wise is today's young person who turns, not to his or her own selfish desires, but to God for answers about the questions of marriage, a career, and children. Since the time of Rachel, the essential values have not changed, nor has God changed. He is still the same great spirit, the invisible image who created our universe and guides it. God's world is one of beauty, not ugliness, one of faith, hope, and love, not fear, hopelessness, and hate.

We are all tested in one way or another every day of our lives, and we have to be wise enough to meet well the tests. Wisdom cares for those who seek her.

> "My son [my daughter], if you aspire to be a servant of the
>   Lord,
> prepare yourself for testing.
> Set a straight course, be resolute,
> and do not lose your head in time of disaster.
> Hold fast to him, never desert him,
> if you would end your days in prosperity.
> Bear every hardship that is sent you;
> be patient under humiliation, whatever the cost.
> For gold is assayed by fire,

and the Lord proves men [and women] in the furnace of
   humiliation.
Trust him and he will help you;
steer a straight course and set your hope on him"

(Ecclesiasticus 2:1-6, NEB).

Chapter 6

A Mother Ever Near:
Jochebed

(Exod. 2:1–10; 6:20)

The wise mother is the first to recognize exceptional promise in her child. Jochebed, the mother of Moses, was the first to perceive she had borne a child of destiny. When the pharaoh decreed that all newborn Israelite sons be killed, she saved her baby by putting him in a handmade cradle near the banks of the Nile River.

When the pharaoh's daughter went there to bathe and came upon this beautiful baby, she sent one of her maids to bring it to her. Although she was startled to find the child by himself, she soon learned he was not alone. His young sister Miriam stood nearby watching, serving as both nurse and spokesman. His mother, who had arranged this protection, was not far away herself, near enough to hear his cries.

Miriam asked the pharaoh's daughter, "Shall I go and call you a nurse from the Hebrew women to nurse the child for you?" Pharaoh's daughter answered, "Go." So the girl went and called his mother.

And pharaoh's daughter told Jochebed, "Take this child away and nurse him for me, and I will give you your wages" (Exod. 2:9). So Jochebed took the child and nursed him (probably in the palace) and taught him the wisdom of his own people.

Moses grew up as the adopted son of the pharaoh's daughter and was educated in the Egyptian manner. But Jochebed, like her son, had a foreordained role to fulfill. She rejoiced that she could give her son a mother's love and tenderness during his formative years.

Out of the endlessly rocking cradle comes the miracle of love between mother and child, a love first conceived between two parents. With a sense of wonder the world respects the miracle of a promising child, brought forth in love and gently nurtured by the mother. The Jewish people have a saying: "God could not be everywhere, and therefore he made mothers."

The question has been asked, "What are Raphael's madonnas but the shadow of a mother's love, fixed in permanent outline forever?"

Henry Wadsworth Longfellow reminds us that "Even He that died for us upon the cross, in the last hour, in the agony of death, was mindful of his mother, as if to teach us that this holy love should be our last worldly thought—the last point of earth from which the soul should take its flight from heaven."

The mother's warm body is the point at which the living being enters the consciousness of the material world. That is why Mary, the mother of the Christ, sang, "My soul doth magnify the Lord."

A revolution is under way in our technological era, and it centers around whether a mother should work outside the home. Thousands of mothers have no choice, for they must sustain their children by their own labor. However, what matters most is that a mother take the time to love and inspire her child. The mother's blessing is important even to the end of a child's life.

Soon after George Washington took office, he called on his eighty-year-old mother, Mary Ball Washington, and she bade him goodbye, saying, "Go, fulfill the high destiny which heaven appears to assign you; go and may heaven's and your mother's blessing be with you always."

Abraham Lincoln, never forgetting the inspiration of his mother, said, "All I am or hope to be I owe to my angel mother." This could be applied to his own mother, Nancy, as well as to his stepmother, Sarah, whom he loved dearly.

Because of our changing needs, few parents today can be as dedicated as Jochebed or as the little-known mother who inspired Margaret Widdemer's poem, "The Watcher."

> She always learned to watch for us,
>   anxious if we were late
> In winter by the window,
>   in summer by the gate;

And though we mocked her tenderly,
   who had such foolish care,
The long way home would seem more safe
   Because she waited there.

Her thoughts were all so full of us—
   she never could forget
And so I think that where she is
   she must be watching yet,

Waiting till we come home to her,
   Anxious if we are late—
Watching from heaven's window,
   Leaning from heaven's gate.

With parents like "The Watcher," few children grow to be problem adults. They will have problems, that is certain, but they will meet them with more confidence and faith.

Chapter 7

The Property Rights
of Women:
The Five Sisters and Moses

(Num. 26:33, 27:1–11; 36:10)

"Our father died in the wilderness in a righteous cause, Why should the name of our father disappear because he had no sons? We feel we should be given our father's tribal inheritance along with his brothers," spoke the five sisters to Moses after the death of their father Zelophehad.

Moses meditated on their request, during which God said to him, "If a man dies, and has no son, then you shall give his inheritance to his daughters along with his brothers." And this became a statute and an ordinance written into the civil laws of Israel. Even after the marriage of these five sisters to the sons of Manasseh, the son of Joseph, their inheritance remained in the tribe of the family of their father, which means that they retained community property separate from that belonging to their husbands.

This is the first case on record in which specific women attained their property rights in an open court. It is easy to suppose that this father had instilled into his five daughters a rare spirit, a knowledge of the laws set up by Moses, and a willingness to stand up for their rights.

Why were they so successful? First, they made their plea before a fair-minded religious and civil leader who regarded both men and women as children of God. Next, they approached him not as inferior human beings but as well-informed persons. Finally, they knew they were right, and they spoke to Moses, not in defiance, but with reason. They were polite, deliberate, and positive in their approach. Their argument could not be denied by one so just as Moses. He must have heard again and again an echo of their voices, interrogating him with such questions as, "Why should the name of our father disappear because he has no son?"

Because of the justice of their cause these five sisters not only helped themselves but those who came after them. Their confidence in the laws set up by Moses still benefits women. In his first address Moses said to the people, "You shall not be partial in judgment; you shall hear the small and the great alike; you shall not be afraid of the face of man, for the judgment is God's; and the case that is too hard for you, you shall bring to me, and I will hear it" (Deut. 1:17).

God is no respecter of persons. He made women different from men but not inferior to them. With Christ came a faith that was superior to the law. His new covenant made it clear that in him, men and women, are the children of God through faith. Paul declared, "There is neither Jew nor Greek, there is neither slave nor free, there is neither male nor female; for you are all one in Christ Jesus. And if you are Christ's, then you are . . . heirs according to the promise" (Gal. 3:28-29).

Christ saw men and women as people; he did not favor one sex over the other but saw both as heirs of salvation, promise, faith, and righteousness and as joint heirs according to the hope of eternal life. Heirs of salvation are women and men who inherit peace and reconciliation with God—through a right relationship with God in Christ. But as inheritors of so great a gift, they must be prepared to accept its demands.

We are all joint heirs of promise and hope in eternal life. As for faith what is more to be desired, a woman with a firm step that walks in faith, or an uncertain step that staggers in expensive shoes?

The legacy of being an heir to a fifth gift, namely Righteousness, is vitally important to women, the standard bearers of the race. Think what it means to be clothed with Righteousness! Outer garments are of little significance compared to the inner garments, best described as things of the Spirit. How blessed is the woman who places greater value on these than on elegant brocades, furs and expensive jewels.

Who is more admired, the woman who receives every nickel

she fights for, or God's kind of woman, described in Prov. 31: 10-31? The latter neither seeks honors nor demands recognition. She is not disturbed about her human rights, but she merits many. Because she does, her children call her blessed, her husband praises her, and she has the support of all the people in the city gates. What woman could desire more?

Chapter 8

A Liberated Woman: *Miriam*

(Exod. 15:20–21; Num. 12:1–16)

Miriam, the devoted, distinguished sister of Moses, stood in the vanguard of liberated women in ancient times when she, along with Moses and her brother Aaron, led the community of Israel out of centuries of Egyptian bondage. As they crossed the Red Sea, its surging waters miraculously parted and then closed in on the pharaoh, following behind with his chariots and horsemen.

At the time of the liberation Miriam was young and full of the spirit of God. One can still hear echoes of her timbrels as she danced and sang, "Sing to the Lord, for he has triumphed gloriously; the horse and his rider he has thrown into the sea" (Gen. 15:21). Miriam inspired the other women of Israel with her joyous spirit. Free at last from the long oppression of the unjust pharaohs, Miriam signified a new kind of liberation for women. Her leadership heralded the advent of Israel's heroic age, when women as well as men rose up to declare their freedom.

Miriam sensed a renewal of mind and spirit in the great victory she shared with her brothers. This triumph established her role as one of Israel's noble women.

Several decades later, Miriam's personality took a strange twist. She disapproved of Moses' marriage to a Cushite (Ethiopian), probably a black woman. Miriam, who had shown such love for Moses when he was a baby and when as a young man he led his people to victory, began to rebuke him publicly. Her reaction completely contradicted her earlier support of Moses when he led Israel across the Red Sea, when he talked with God on Mount Sinai, or when he set up Israel's first civil and religious laws. Miriam then looked up to her brother as the honored leader of Israel. When she reproached him and attempted to become the arbiter of his personal affairs, she jeopardized his authority over Israel.

"Has the Lord indeed spoken only through Moses? Has he not spoken through us [she and Aaron] also?" (Num. 12:2), Miriam asked.

After a personal encounter with God, Moses and Aaron pondered God's words; "My servant Moses is entrusted with all my house. With him I speak clearly. Why then were you not afraid to speak against him?" God questioned Aaron as well as Miriam, for Aaron had been copartner in criticizing Moses.

After this, Miriam was stricken with leprosy, but she was to learn again, as she had at the Red Sea, that God is not a God of wrath but a God of love.

When Aaron saw his sister suddenly turn white as snow, he cried out, "Oh, my Lord, do not punish us because we have done foolishly and have sinned. Do not let her die," he begged.

The tolerant, ever-helpful Moses prayed, "Heal, her, O God, I beseech you." And later Miriam was healed.

In her suffering she probably realized that she had been unloving and unwise in her actions toward Moses and that she was more arrogant than credible when she put herself ahead of the Lord before whom Moses had drawn so close at Mount Sinai. Her new perception probably helped her to see that she was in bondage to herself or she would not have sought to place Moses in bondage to her. Actually she belittled herself when she tried to belittle her brother. She knew she must draw close to God, as she had been when she and her people had sung so joyfully:

> "The Lord is my strength and my song,
>> and he has become my salvation:
> this is my God, and I will praise him,
>> my father's God and I will exalt him" (Exod. 15:1-2).

Miriam did not forget the ethical instruction given to Moses by God in one of the laws of his covenant with Israel: "You shall not utter a false report" (Exod. 23:1).

In the last part of her life Miriam became selfish, complacent, fearful, and unloving toward Moses. She who had known bondage, then liberty, then God's abundance, re-entered bondage. Gone were the spiritual faith, courage, and freedom that had made her a young heroine of Israel.

The wonder of the Bible is that Miriam continues to serve as a model to contemporary men and women, both in her achievements and in her failures.

Miriam's sudden fall reminds us that we have to guard our thoughts constantly, or we too can be in bondage before we know it, not only to ourselves but to our careers, debts, possessions, and sometimes pursuits that lead us away from God.

> "I strove for wisdom with all my might,
> and was scrupulous in whatever I did. . . .
> I set my heart on possessing wisdom,
> and by keeping myself pure I found her.
> With her I gained understanding from the first;
> therefore I shall never be at a loss.
> Because I passionately yearned to discover her,
> I won a noble prize" (Ecclesiasticus 51:19-21, NEB).

Miriam did not find real fulfillment in her later life. And neither will we unless we have learned to live apart from self and for others, have served our community, nation and family, and have learned to manage our home well and to worship in the beauty of holiness.

Chapter 9

No Patience at All:
Job's Wife

(Job 2:9; 31:9–12; 28:20, 23–28)

"Curse God, and die," spoke Job's wife to her husband, who was afflicted with loathsome sores from the soles of his feet to the crown of his head.

"You speak as one of the foolish women would speak. Shall we receive good at the hand of God, and shall we not also receive evil?" Job asked his wife (Job 2:9-10).

In his physical and mental suffering Job had untiring patience; his wife had none. Her problems were much the same as his: the loss of all their children—seven sons and three daughters—and all their wealth. But pain placed an added burden on her, for no woman is a whole person when her husband is burdened with many afflictions.

Job's wife, however, was blessed but did not know it, for no matter what happened to Job, he continued to acknowledge God, his creator and redeemer. He never doubted God's goodness, even when he was treated as a stranger by all those about him: wife, intimate friends, kinfolk, house guests, little children, maidservants. He was still able to say that a sovereign God does as he pleases with the righteous and wicked alike.

Amid criticisms from friends, Job held fast to his righteousness. He still declared, "I will not let God go." Finally he concluded that God is never unjust, that he uses pain to chasten.

This belief contrasts with that of his wife, whose one statement, "Curse God and die," flows through her brief biography like a polluted stream. However, Job's reaction to his wife is an example of how we are to relate to men and women who are impatient, unloving, and unkind. Instead of criticizing his wife for her unkindness, Job set forth to analyze his obligations as a husband.

> "If ever my heart was enticed by
>   women,
>   if ever I haunted my neighbour's
>   door,
>   may my own wife be a slave to
>   strangers,
>   a concubine for other men!
> Adultery would be an infamous
>   offence,
>   a crime that calls for punishment;
>   it is a fire that burns life to a
>   cinder,
>   it would burn up whatever I
>   possess." (Job 31:9-12, Moffatt).

There is no further reference to the attitude of Job's wife toward her husband, but, in all fairness to her, she must have remained true to him. In the grand finale of the Book of Job many blessings surround Job's family, more than he had before. Among these are beautiful daughters and sons to take the place of the ones killed earlier in a great wind that swept across the wilderness.

It is likely that Job's wife was the mother of his second set of children. When Job declared, "I will not let God go," his wife probably was wise enough to seek to develop that oneness with God too, as expressed by Job in one of the most profound explanations of wisdom in the Bible.

> "Whence then comes wisdom?
>   And where is the place of understanding? . . .
> God understands the way to it,
>   and he knows its place
> For he looks to the ends of the earth,
>   and sees everything under the heavens.
> When he gave to the wind its weight,
>   and meted out the waters by measure;
> when he made a decree for the rain,
>   and a way for the lightning of the thunder;
> then he saw it and declared it;
>   he established it, and searched it out.
> And he said to man,
> 'Behold, the fear of the Lord, that is wisdom;
>   and to depart from evil is understanding'" (Job 28:20, 23-28).

Section II
A Life of Fulfillment

When a woman finds fulfillment in the many areas of good living, she becomes a total person, even amid sorrows, failures, disappointments, and heartaches. She learns that the so-called good life is made up of all of these components.

In various ways Old Testament women sought and found real fulfillment. No mother in the Old Testament reveals dedication as much as Hannah, the mother of Samuel. In her great song of praise, often referred to as having influenced Mary's Magnificat, Hannah rises to heights of unselfishness. Deborah reached fulfillment in patriotic service when she led the army of Israel against a powerful enemy that had threatened to annihilate her little country. Jephthah's daughter, a young woman of honor, thought not of herself, in order to fulfill her father's vow. She willingly offered her life as a sacrifice, as was common in ancient times.

Huldah's spiritual awareness helped her guide others spiritually. King Josiah, less prepared, benefited from her womanly insight, as did all the people of Israel after she identified the scrolls found in the temple during a period of restoration.

Fulfillment in a woman's life is expressed in this section also, in daughters of grace and beauty; in the excellent homemaker, who found her greatest joy in her home; in the hospitable woman, who gave out love to all who crossed her household.

Finally, devout women in the Bible find their greatest spiritual satisfaction in worship when they experience at first hand the beauty of holiness, as delineated in the last chapter in this section.

Chapter 10

Mother and Child:
Hannah and Samuel

(1 Sam. 1, 2)

"O Lord of hosts, if thou wilt not . . . forget thy maidservant, but wilt give to thy maidservant a son, then I will give him to the Lord all the days of his life" (1 Sam. 1:11).

This is the vow that Hannah, mother of Samuel, made to God in the tabernacle at Shiloh, where she and her husband Elkanah went with their family to pray. The next day Hannah and her family—which included her husband's secondary wife, Penninah, and her children—went back to the tabernacle to worship. After they returned home to Ramah, a village close by, Hannah conceived and gave birth to Samuel. Although Hannah later had other children, three sons and two daughters, Samuel was the inspiration for her song of praise (1 Sam. 2:1-10). When she had weaned him, she took him back to the tabernacle, where she said she "lent" him to the Lord. There Samuel ministered to the Lord under the guidance of the priest Eli, and the Bible says "he grew in the presence of the Lord."

Hannah seems to tell us that when a woman fully consecrates herself to motherhood and dedicates her child to God, nobler children are born, children who can help raise the standards of the world, strengthen the weak, and exalt the strong. Hannah and Samuel typify the best in the mother-child relationship in the Old Testament. Hannah passed on to us a special legacy of tenderness, protectiveness, love, and purity between mother and child. The words of Samuel's father Elkanah suggest that Hannah had his cooperation. An old text of Samuel, found in the Quamran Cave, suggests that Elkanah was with Hannah and probably knelt beside her when she prayed in the tabernacle for a son.

Hannah probably did not live to see Samuel become one of Israel's great men of destiny, the first of the prophets after Moses and the last of the judges. Samuel had the honor of anointing David as king, and he is still held in high respect by Jews, Muslims, and Christians.

Hannah stands worlds apart from mothers and fathers who don't care, who accept abortion as a way out of responsibility, and who place sexual gratification ahead of parenthood. The child, Samuel, stands in sharp contrast to the lonely, disillusioned children who have no sense of destiny and no identity, and who lack parents to love or be loved by. Such children "pass through the world like straws upon a river, which are carried the way the stream and winds drive them." This is Susannah Wesley's apt description of those human beings who fail to seek the presence of a God who, as she relates, "is about our beds and about our paths and spies out all our ways."

Many great men and women have attested to the natural affinity that exists between a mother and a child who love each other. No one in literature has written with deeper feeling about a mother's love for her newborn infant than the French novelist Honoré de Balzac (1799-1850).

A ray of light pierced the darkness; my heart and soul, my inner self—a self I had never known before [came forth] . . . as a flower bursts its sheath at the first warm kiss of the sun. It was at the moment when the little wretch fastened on my breast and sucked. Not even the sensation of the child's first cry was so exquisite as this. This is the dawn of motherhood. . . .

The sensation which rises from it, and which penetrates to the very core of my life, belies all description. . . . To bear a child is nothing; to nourish it is birth renewed every hour.

There is no caress of a lover with half the power of those little pink hands, as they stray about, seeking whereby to lay hold on life. . . . what dreams come to us as we watch the clinging nursling. All our powers, whether of mind or body, are at its service. . . . A child is tied to our heartstrings, as the spheres are linked to their creator; we cannot think of God except as a mother's heart written large. . . .

For myself, dear soul, I grow happier and happier every moment. Each hour creates a fresh tie between the mother and her infant. The very nature of my feelings proves to me that they are normal, permanent, indestructible.
From *To Mother with Love,* edited by Frederick Ungar, Stephen Daye, 1951.

Literature abounds with tributes to mothers. The greater the creativity of the child, the greater the adoration of the mother, an adoration that goes from the mother out to God himself. In the child's search for achievement in adulthood, he or she reaches out to an illimitable creative power linked to and through the mother.

In his anthology *Letters to Mother* (Great Neck, N.Y.: Channel Press, 1959), Charles Van Doren has letters that fascinating men and women, explorers, poets, philosophers, statesmen, musicians, wrote to their mothers. The key of appreciation that runs through these letters is especially noteworthy, and the book's dedication to the author's mother is no exception. "I owe you life, the most valuable of all gifts. I cannot repay it with a book, yet this one is dedicated to you with love, which makes all gifts possible."

One of the most amazing statements comes from the American jurist, Louis Brandeis (1856-1941). "I believe, most beloved mother, that the improvement of the world reform can only arise when mothers like you are increased thousands of times and have more children," pgs. 123-124.

One of the most amazing letters was penned by Harry Truman, when he lovingly shared with his mother the highest moment of his life. He recounted it in April 1945, after President Roosevelt's sudden death. This letter first appears in his book, Memoirs of Harry Truman, Years of Decisions, Vol. 1 (New York, Doubleday, 1956).

It was the only time in my life, I think, that I ever felt as if I'd had a real shock. I had hurried to the White House to see the President, and when I arrived, I found I was the President. No one in the history of our country ever had it happen to him just that way. (*Letters to Mothers,* p. 303).

On her fiftieth birthday Susan B. Anthony (1820-1906), the American abolitionist and suffragette, wrote her mother:

> In the last few hours I have lived over nearly all of life's struggle. The most painful is the memory of my mother's long and weary efforts to get her six children up into womanhood and manhood. My thoughts center on your struggles. ... I can see the old home—the brick makers—the dinner pails—the sick mother—the few years of more fear than hope in the new house, and the hard years since. And yet with it all, I know there was an undercurrent of joy and love which makes the summing-up vastly in their favor.
>
> My constantly recurring thought and prayer now are that the coming fraction of the century, whether it be small or large, may witness nothing less worthy in my life than has the half just closed—that no word or act of mine may lessen its weight in the scale of truth and right. (Ida Husted Harper, *The Life and Works of Susan B. Anthony,* Vol. 1, Indianapolis: Bobbs-Merrill Co., p. 234.)

Every letter in the Charles Van Doren book, from Truman's "Dear Mama" letter to the "Beloved Mother" letter of Justice Brandeis, expresses the miracle of love between a mother and her adult child. All of life seems to have been more wondrous to both because of this relationship, so impressively recorded in the story of Hannah and her son Samuel.

Chapter 11

A National Heroine:
Deborah

(Judg. 4, 5)

> "Rise up, you women who are at ease, hear my voice;
>   you complacent daughters, give ear to my speech. . . .
> until the Spirit is poured upon us from on high" (Isa. 32:9, 15).

When spirit-filled, fearless women rise up out of obscurity to defend their nation in time of insecurity, they may become national heroines. Such a women was Deborah, who led the army of Israel to victory many centuries before Christ. She is the Bible's most inspiring example of how the nation of Israel was saved in time of lethargy by the creativity, initiative, courage, and spiritual perception of one woman.

Deborah arose to leadership, not on her own, but on the will of the people when Israel's safety was threatened by the powerful Canaanite, King Jabin. His commander-in-chief, Sisera, with his nine hundred chariots of iron, had intimidated Israel for twenty years, and the people feared to go against him in battle. The spiritual leaders prayed for help, and the answer came forth in Deborah, the wife of a little-known man, Lappidoth.

Deborah held court, as it were, at a place called Deborah's Palm Tree, between Ramah and Bethel in the hill country of Ephraim. In her life and work, Deborah, a judge and a prophet, is one of the greatest heroines in the Old Testament. Because she was a wise woman, the Israelites came to her for counsel in settling their disputes. Among those with whom she counseled was Barak, once a prisoner of the powerful Canaanites but now fearful of an encounter with them. Deborah gave Barak courage, however, to marshal ten thousand men and to bring them to the slope of Mount Tabor. "Go, the Lord God of Israel commands you," Deborah told Barak.

"Now is the time for action!" she assured him.

Barak answered, "If you will go with me, I will go; but if you will not go with me, I will not go."

"I will surely go with you," she said, "nevertheless, the road on which you are going will not lead to your glory, for the Lord will sell Sisera into the hand of a woman" (Judg. 4:8-9).

Deborah then set forth for battle with the fearful Barak, giving him strength every step of the way. Aided by the weather and the swollen Kishon River, Deborah leading in one direction and Barak in another defeated the Canaanites.

The account of the battle is climaxed with the war song of Deborah and Barak, one of the oldest folk epics of Israel. In this thrilling victory song, Deborah is triumphant as she sings, "I will make melody to the Lord, the God of Israel." Then she chants on:

> "From heaven fought the stars,
>   from their courses they fought against Sisera.
> The torrent Kishon swept them away,
>   the onrushing torrent, the torrent Kishon.
> March on, my soul with might!" (Judg. 5:20-21).

At the end Deborah sings of the defeat of the greedy mother who sits waiting for the return of Sisera, her son, but as Deborah prophesied, Sisera has already been killed by a woman, Jael.

This mother did not know this yet; so she sat peering out of the window, asking:

> "Why is his chariot so long in coming?
>   Why tarry the hoofbeats of his chariots?
> Her wisest ladies make answer,
>   nay, she gives answer to herself,
> 'Are they not finding and dividing the spoil?—
>   A maiden or two for every man?' " (Judg. 5:28-30).

She was awaiting fine embroidered gifts for herself brought back as spoils from Israel.

What a vast difference in these two women—the greedy mother of Sisera, who cried for the spoils of war as well as the safety of her son, and Deborah, "a mother of Israel," who made melody to God in a triumphant victory song.

Public-spirited women through the centuries have tried to emulate Deborah, a prophetess and a judge in Israel. Today we women need to analyze our objectives and goals, patterning them, not after the greedy mother of Sisera, but after the unselfish Deborah, whose song still rings forth: "March, on my soul, with might!" She who blessed God before and after victory teaches us that in times of national danger and distress women can be great catalysts for good.

Our prayer should be, "God give us fearless women who bring restoration out of calamity and who learn to sing with the Psalmist,"

> "Though a host encamp against me,
>   my heart shall not fear;
> though war arise against me,
>   yet I will be confident." (Ps. 27:3).

Chapter 12

A Child with Honor:
Jephthah's Daughter

(Judg. 11:1–2, 29–40)

"My father, if you have made a promise to the Lord, do to me according to your promise, now that the Lord has given you victory over your enemies the Ammonites," spoke Jephthah's daughter to her father.

"You have made a vow to the Lord. You must keep it. Do not fall down on your vow for me. Let me alone two months, that I may go and wander on the mountains and bewail my virginity, I and my companions." And Jephthah's daughter went away for two months and then returned to her father. He kept his vow, which was, "If you will give the Ammonites into my hand, then whoever comes forth from the doors of my house to meet me, when I return victorious shall be the Lord's, and I will offer him up for a burnt offering."

Often children fall behind their parents in their mores, stamina, and achievements. But in every generation one or two children in a family rise up to support the weaknesses of other members of the family. Such a child was the unnamed daughter of Jephthah, "a mighty man of valor," whose father was a distinguished Hebrew and whose mother was a harlot. Jephthah stood tall as commander of the army and in his devotion to his only daughter.

She excelled in her morality, in her heroic effort to retain purity, even to death, and finally in her willingness to offer herself either as a burnt offering or to the dedicated life of a celibate in the sanctuary in order to give her father freedom in keeping his pledge to God. He never realized that he would be called upon to sacrifice his beloved daughter, who would rush to greet him when he returned home victorious from battle.

Jephthah was ready to renege on his solemn pledge, but his daughter would not permit him to do so. Her father's honor came above her own pleasures; so she resigned herself to what was best for her father, not to her own happiness.

Honor such as this comes at a high price. Jephthah's daughter was more honorable than her father or her grandmother, and because she was, she became precious in God's sight. Shakespeare had much to say about honor, and Jephthah's daughter lived up to what this great English writer wrote hundreds of centuries later: "Mine honor is my life; both grow in one; take honor from me and my life is done."

Jephthah's daughter gave her life, but she retained her honor, which survives longer than any lifetime.

Chapter 13

Spiritual Awareness:
Huldah

(2 Kings 22:14–20; 2 Chron. 34:14–33)

A spiritually perceptive woman can see into hearts and human situations to which the average person is blind. Such a person was Huldah, a Hebrew prophetess during the reign of King Josiah.

When an ancient scroll of the Book of Law, sections of which are now part of the Book of Deuteronomy, was uncovered by workmen during a restoration of the Temple at Jerusalem, no one in the kingdom, not even the king, knew what the scroll contained or whether it was authentic. So Josiah sent it by his high priest and other messengers to one of the best-educated women in the realm, Huldah, the wife of Shallum, who supervised the palace tailor shop.

In ancient times, important records were often sealed into the walls of the Temple for safekeeping. This one was of special significance because it probably included the core of what became the first book of the Bible to be canonized.

Huldah, who must have been either a teacher or a preacher, had a spiritual insight that took her into the hidden mysteries of God, a realm few others presumed to enter. Her secret was her love for God. Like the prophets, Huldah prefaced the message she sent back to King Josiah, not with her own appraisal, but with this positive affirmation:

"Thus says the Lord, the God of Israel: Regarding the words which you have heard, because your heart was penitent, and you humbled yourself before the Lord, . . . I also have heard you, says the Lord. . . . I will gather you [Josiah] to your fathers, and you . . . to your grave in peace, and your eyes shall not see all the evil which I will bring upon this place" (2 Kings 22:18-20).

This is only a part of the message Huldah sent back to King Josiah, who believed her prophecy. Immediately he began to use this lost book as an instrument of reform in Israel. Because it is now thought to be the brilliant work of a group of prophets, priests, and other spiritual giants who recorded the ideals of their nation in this scroll, he did not go wrong in following it to the letter.

Huldah's bold, penetrating message seemed to interpret the mind of God to King Josiah. She was certain God had called her to speak. Her distinctive power was recognized, not only in her spiritual perception, but in the way she acted upon her opportunity to use it. Huldah's prophecy takes us into another dimension of time, and we wonder at the spiritual awareness of this woman of more than twenty-six centuries ago. Another phase of the miracle is that a king took the time to listen to a woman.

Is there a woman in our time who could make such correct predictions into the future that they would survive through the twenty-six centuries to come? If so, will it be about a matter that so concerns an entire nation that it will be put into action by a great head of government? Will our age produce a woman with such a deep knowledge of God that she has the ability to recognize what is good and right and God-given for our nation?

Since parts of this lost book are still found in Deuteronomy, it could be that through its timeless message we hear more clearly the following refrain, which is so appropriate to our world today: "So you shall keep the commandments of the Lord your God, by walking in his ways and by fearing him. For the Lord your God is bringing [or has brought] you into a good land, a land of brooks of water, of fountains and springs, flowing forth in valleys and hills, a land of wheat and barley, of vines and fig trees and pomegranates, a land of olive trees and honey, a land in which you will eat bread without scarcity, in which you will lack nothing, a land whose stones are iron, and out of whose hills you can dig copper. And you shall eat and be full, and you shall bless the Lord your God for the good land he has given you" (Deut. 8:6-10).

We in America have been blessed far more than little Israel at the time of Josiah and Huldah. Our garners are so full that we waste almost as much as we use, and we have enough to divide liberally with other countries. Technology is opening up avenues of thought never dreamed of before. Diseases, such as smallpox and polio, have been conquered. In the daytime our cities burst with activity. At night, as we fly above them, they resemble celestial bodies.

We are prone to forget, however, who brought us to this good land and what God does require of us, which is to love him, and to keep his statutes an commandments. These spell blessings beyond our fondest imagination, but if we fail God, these blessings can vanish. Huldah's words still exhort us to be attuned to God's Word, which never changes.

Chapter 14

Radiance . . . in Daughters:
Of Grace and Beauty

(Ps. 144:12–13, 15)

In his description of a "truly happy land where Jehovah is God," the psalmist wrote:

> "May our sons in their youth
> be like plants full grown,
> our daughters like corner pillars
> cut for the structure of a palace" (Ps. 144:12).

What can spell greater happiness than having daughters of such grace and beauty that they suggest the sculptured pillars of a palace? This psalm, pulsating with a peaceful rhythm, also invokes God:

> "May our garners be full
> providing all manner of store;
> may our sheep bring forth thousands
> and ten thousands in our fields. . . .
> Happy the people to whom such blessings fall!
> happy the people whose God is the Lord!" (Ps. 144:13, 15).

A radiant daughter is a valuable asset to a mother and father, but the radiance of daughters must come from an inner beauty. Such beauty takes in the fruits of the spirit: love, joy, tranquillity, patience, gentleness, goodness, faithfulness, meekness, and self-control.

Every little girl born into the world is a gift of God. What she makes of her life depends upon her background, her training, and the standards by which she lives. Radiance can not be preserved for tomorrow with a camera or painted with subtle colors on a canvas. It is neither easily attained nor guaranteed for all of a woman's life.

The basic element of spiritual radiance is an indefinable light. Paul described attaining this kind of light when he wrote, "Be aglow with the Spirit, serve the Lord" (Rom. 12:11). If a woman is disciplined and unselfish, if she lives close to God, her face can glow through all the years of her life.

Whatever a young woman becomes stems from how she accepts suffering, how she lives for others, how she disciplines herself, how much she loves, and how much she depends on the divinity within. A young girl said to her mother after a beautiful, mature visitor had left their home, "I wish I could grow old like that, gentle, serene, lovable." The discerning and quick-witted mother replied, "Well, if you want to be that kind of older woman, you had best begin now. She does not impress me as a piece of work that was done in a hurry."

A woman is radiant in her later years if she has used time wisely. She has found time to work (the price of success), think (the source of power), read (the foundation of knowledge), pray (the way to serenity), think of others (the road to joy), laugh heartily (the music of the soul), rejoice in goodness, and light a flame of sympathy and tenderness (the real radiance of true femininity).

Chapter 15

Home Management:
The Excellent Homemaker

(Prov. 31: 13–19, 21–22, 24, 27)

Ten of the twenty-two verses on the excellent woman in Proverbs praise her skill as a homemaker. Nothing in ancient or modern literature sets a higher standard for the homemaker than this passage. The excellent homemaker creates a home that is a refuge for all who enter, a sanctuary to which others turn in time of joy and sorrow. She brings forth with her own hands visual pleasures in her garden and delectable meals at her table. Like a refreshing balm, comforts and beauty surround her guests. She is neither enslaved nor denigrated by her work in the home, where members of her family live, trust, dream, and love.

The excellent homemaker seeks to handle her resources wisely. Because she is a good manager, she will never fear want in the future, for she is certain that God will provide for all her needs. However, she remembers that there is no excuse for idleness, that work is a blessing, and that discipline is her way of life; so she manages well what she has, reminding us that the important thing is not how much we have but how well we manage what we do have.

She rises before dawn to prepare breakfast for her household and plans the day's work for her home helpers. She finds wool and flax and busily spins them into cloth. She goes out to inspect a piece of property and buys it if she thinks it is a good investment. She gathers grapes from her vineyards, both to feed her household and to sell in the marketplace. She is an energetic worker, who thinks nothing of toiling far into the night to achieve her goals.

Wisdom built her house; so it cannot fall. Though all who come into her presence may not tell her, they know and feel that her wisdom is from God and that she is refreshed continually "like water from a mountain spring." She watches over her household as if it were a successful business. She learns to cope with anything, for the fear of the Lord is her lamp. Her dwelling is never without light. It is all about her—in her candles, in her heart, in all that she says and does.

What modern woman has more? What woman sets her goals so high and achieves them at harder labor? Or who finds greater joy in the achievement itself? Such homes are still about us, most often in the most unexpected places. They are not always in the more affluent areas, where professional decorators come, but are often on quiet, shaded streets, where life is lived simply and calmly.

Page Smith, author of the prize-winning biography *John Adams,* wrote skillfully about such a home in a newspaper article.

To the Los Angeles Times:

Dear women's liberationists, I wished your liberation before many of you felt yourselves enslaved. I urged "the case for male dishwashing" a decade before it became a cause, or a clause in marriage contracts. I wish you every good thing in the world. If desperate necessity drives you to work, I wish you work more interesting and rewarding than that most men engage in—and certainly equal pay and equal opportunities.

But desist, I beg you, from denigrating the home. That is where I live and where, I trust, you live. I wish you, as the best legacy of all, its joys and delights.

Do not depict the home as the prison to escape from, for you will find that your home is you—as surely as it is your husband and your children—and none of us can escape, finally, from ourselves.

There is only one environment where most of us have any control at all—our home. There we create the environment and set the tone. It is the one place where we enact the drama of our own reality, where we are ourselves, free of those debilitating distortions of reality that most of us experience as our "work."

The flight from home is thus a flight from ourselves—from our own barrenness, inattention, unimaginativeness, unlovingness—to the spiritually numbing distractions of most jobs and careers, to a world of ceaseless motion, restlessness, misplaced ardor, false hopes, all the illusions of power and success of which our culture is so prolific.

Today, nevertheless, the home—which should be a center of peace and joy, of the classic domestic delights that have sustained life for centuries—is depicted as a prison cell, the abode of a boredom only slightly relieved by the pale blue flicker of television; or, more commonly perhaps, by a bedlam of squabbling children, unmade beds and unwashed dishes, presided over by a mad housewife, tranquilized twice daily, tending to dipsomania.

I don't want to "condemn" anyone to the home, man or woman. But I have a settled conviction that a man's and a woman's place is in the home. I have spent as much of my life in mine as I could. I leave it reluctantly; I return to it joyfully. I can hardly persuade my wife to leave it at all.

She has made it into such a splendid refuge, such a magnificent nest resplendent with visual treasures, with aesthetic delights, with surprises, joys, comforts as can hardly be imagined. The most ingenious and beneficent employer, lavish as Croesus, could not do a tenth as well, concludes Page Smith, who tells us that Abigail Adams used to complain to John that he and his colleagues in the Continental Congress talked glibly enough of liberty but failed to extend its benefits to their wives. The charge has been often repeated, never more frequently than at present.

Should we as homemakers ever forget there are two divine institutions in the world, the church and the home? The home is God's as truly as is the church, and should be a lighthouse to the community. The keeper of the lighthouse is the homemaker. No nation is stronger than its homemakers.

Napoleon marching with all his armies destroyed. Hitler with all of his ambitions murdered millions. Croesus with all his wealth subjugated many of his neighbors. But the home builder in whatever century she lives, from the time of the excellent and wise Woman of Proverbs to the present, is a queen in her own right.

Chapter 16

Hospitality:
An Expression of Love

*The Shunammite (2 Kings 4:8-13), Mary and Martha (Luke 10:38-42),
Mary, Mother of John Mark (Acts 12:12), Lydia (Acts 16:15), Priscilla (Acts
18:1-3; 1 Cor. 16:19), 1 Tim. 5:10; Titus 1:8; Heb. 13:2; 1 Pet. 4:9*

"Let us make a small roof chamber with walls, and put there
for him a bed, a table, a chair, and a lamp, so that whenever he
comes to us, he can go in there" (2 Kings 4:10). These were the
hospitable words of the Shunammite woman to her husband
about Elisha, of whom she further spoke, "I perceive that he is a
holy man of God, who is continually passing our way" (2 Kings
4:9).

After she and her husband set up the room, the prophet
Elisha came for rest and meditation.

It was probably an upper room reached by an outer stairway
from the garden. No matter how tired Elisha might be after
traveling from one village to another, as he ministered to others,
he was assured a room of his own. It awaited him in the home of
this "great woman," as she was called, and her husband.

The discerning Elisha soon saw that this couple wanted a son
in their childless home but had given up hope of having one. He
assured them that a son was forthcoming, and the following
spring the Shunammite woman gave birth to a son, the first of
many blessings Elisha brought into this hospitable home.

The second blessing came several years later when Elisha,
through prayer and artificial respiration, described in 2 Kings
4:34, raised the son from the dead. The Shunammite was so
sure that Elisha was a man of God that she was confident all
would be well in her home if Elisha were near; and it was so.

The words of hospitality from a woman in Bible times represent thoughtfulness and home at best. Coming from the lips of a wealthy and influential woman like the Shunammite, who was great in faith and kindness, they had a lasting influence for good.

Jesus looked forward to visiting the Bethany home of Mary and Martha, the sisters of his friend Lazarus. Martha was such a meticulous homemaker that she often was too busy for outside interests. Jesus once told her that she must not put housekeeping above everything else. He added that Mary, a woman more active in things of the spirit, had chosen the better course; however, Jesus did not discount Martha's solicitude for him as a guest in her home. It took the practicality of Martha and the spirituality of Mary to provide the home environment that Jesus enjoyed. After the death of Lazarus, Mary and Martha drew closer to Jesus in their sorrow, for Lazarus was his dear friend. Their home became a refuge for Jesus' comforting thoughts on the life and the resurrection.

Mary, the mother of John Mark, had a home, said to be in the south end of Mount Zion, where many Christians retreated. It was probably a large hospitable house, where prayer groups met and where, it is thought, Pentecost might have taken place.

It is recorded that when Peter was delivered from the chains that had tied his hands together the first place he made for was this home, "where many were gathered together and were praying." This was also where Rhoda, Mary's home helper, probably one of several in her commodious home, met Peter at the door. When Peter entered, he told the praying group how the Lord had helped him out of prison. Peter must have felt so at home in Mary's house that he rushed there to find immediate surcease from prison bars.

No one was more hospitable than Lydia, the first European convert to Christianity. Paul wrote, "When she was baptized, with her household, she besought us, saying, 'If you have judged me to be faithful to the Lord, come to my house and stay.' And she prevailed upon us" (Acts 16:15).

Priscilla is remembered because she and her husband, Aquila, were hospitable to Paul in their home at Ephesus, where they were tent makers together. Priscilla also was among the first to establish a church of the household, first at Ephesus and later at Rome. These churches of the household lighted the way for the coming of larger church-meeting places.

Lydia, the successful business woman dealing in dyed textiles, must have given liberally to the church of Philippi, for it was in her home on the east-west Egnation highway between Rome and Asia that the church was cradled. Lydia's home was probably near or on the river bank, where Paul and Silas baptized the first converts, chiefly women, of whom Lydia, a Gentile, was one. She, who had been judged faithful by Paul and Silas, must have given to these two men of light the best in hospitality as well as in faith.

The evangelist Philip and his four unmarried daughters had a house at Caesarea on the Mediterranean. It was probably a rendezvous for Luke, who is thought to have written parts of his Gospel and the Book of Acts there. Others of "Paul's company," as they are described, also went to this home on the Mediterranean, where a growing number of early Christians came both for relief when they were in need and for inspiration. These four daughters helped their father expound the words of God in their home to Christian guests.

The idea of hospitable homes spread during Christ's ministry. He was a host and helper on many occasions himself, for example, at the marriage at Cana when he turned the water into wine; and he was a spiritual host when he sat in the center of his disciples at the Last Supper. Here he was the tender shepherd, giving them a foretaste of what his father's many mansions would be like.

After his ascension, hospitality took on even greater importance. Paul told the Roman church not only to practice hospitality but to "welcome one another . . . as Christ has welcomed you, for the glory of God" (Rom. 15:7). A widow, who was not less than sixty years could qualify for pastoral duties, which included showing hospitality to others, relieving the afflicted, and washing the feet of saints.

The idea of sharing hospitality runs on through the Book of Hebrews, which stresses "do not neglect to show hospitality to strangers, for thereby some have entertained angels unawares" (Heb. 13:2). What a challenge for all Christians! Then Peter

admonished, "Practice hospitality ungrudgingly to one another
... in order that in everything God may be glorified through
Jesus Christ" (1 Pet. 11:9-11).

Hospitality was part of being a good steward, of showing gratitude for home itself, and of teaching in that home what is good
and uplifting.

Chapter 17

Worship in Beauty of Holiness:
Women in Tabernacle and Church

(Exod. 35:25, 38:8; 1 Pet. 3:5; Pss. 43:3–4; 73:25–26)

From the time of Moses' first tent tabernacle to the New Testament church of the household, devout women used their talents and skills to serve God at his holy altar. They stitched, sang, and played the tabrets, lyres, and other musical instruments and served as hostesses at the door of these worship centers. For that first movable tent tabernacle, Hebrew women donated their luxuries, such as solid bronze mirrors, which were cast into fixtures for the outer coverings.

These ancient women learned to come before God as members of a great family, a part of the communion of saints. They learned to sing the first psalms, to pray, and to worship the one God molding history to his will.

> "Oh send out thy light and thy truth;
>   let them lead me,
> let them bring me to thy holy hill
>   and to thy dwelling!
> Then I will go to the altar of God,
>   to God my exceeding joy;
> and I will praise thee with the lyre,
>   O God, my God!" (Pss. 43:3–4).

Early Christian women were encouraged to develop "that glorious beauty . . . seen in these holy women of old, who hoped in God," (1 Pet. 3:5), and they established churches of the household. Phoebe, one of the first deaconesses, traveled from her home in Cenchreae, port of Corinth, as the bearer of Paul's

Letter to the Romans. Paul's tribute to Phoebe shows how he valued her service: "I commend to you our sister Phoebe, a deaconess . . . that you may receive her in the Lord as befits the saints, and help her in whatever she may require from you, for she has been a helper of many and of myself as well" (Rom. 16:1-2).

However, Paul honored other women, including Priscilla (a fellow worker), Mary (the last of six Marys in the New Testament), Tryphena and Tryphosa, and the "beloved" Persis—all of whom "worked hard in the Lord." He also honored Julia and other "saints," as he referred to them in Romans 16.

Philip's daughters (Acts 21:9), four in all, helped their father, an evangelist, in his ministry. These daughters had the gift of prophecy and became known as authorities on the activities of the early church. No doubt they learned much from their father, Philip, who preached, healed, and was instrumental in the Ethiopian eunuch's conversion. Philip and his daughters also entertained Paul on his last journey to Jerusalem, when he stopped over in Caesarea. It is thought that Luke, one of Paul's companions on his journey to Caesarea, might have stopped in their house too. It is easy to understand how well versed these four sisters were in the work of the first Christian churches.

Women in the church today have inherited a rich legacy from these saints of old, who in their witness, commitment, loyalty, and service have inspired women since Bible times. Since the Reformation and Renaissance, women of all faiths have gained new status in the church. Inspiration has flowed like a mighty stream from women in cells and cloisters, primitive churches and great cathedrals. No woman ever sought God more fervently than Jeanne Marie Guyon (1648-1717); she lives on today in her writings. This, her song "By Thy Life I Live" still reaches into the hearts of men and women everywhere.

BY THY LIFE I LIVE

I love my God, but with no love of mine,
    For I have none to give;
I love thee, Lord, but all the love is Thine,
    For by Thy life I live.
I am as nothing, and rejoice to be
Emptied and lost and swallowed up in Thee.
Thou, Lord, alone art all Thy children need,
    And there is none beside;

From thee the streams of blessedness
proceed;
In thee the blest abide,
Fountain of life, and all-abounding grace,
Our source, our center, and our dwelling-
place!

Madame Guyon's words inspire us to repeat with the psalmist:

"Whom have I in heaven but thee?
And there is nothing upon
earth that I desire besides thee.
My flesh and my heart may fail,
but God is the strength of my heart and my portion forever" (Ps.
73:25-26).

In her classic work *Worship,* Evelyn Underhill wrote:

The peculiar function of poetry as the carrying medium of a spiritual intuition otherwise unexpressed, is fully seen when we consider the Psalter in relation to our whole religious history. Without it, we could hardly realize the depth and breadth and height of the devotional landscape within which the historic incarnation took place, for it is the gate which admits us to the inner world of Israel's spiritual experience: the world into which Jesus was born, and in which the real preparation of the Gospel was made. Here we recognize the growing-point of the Hebrew spirit of worship; carrying forward the gifts of the past, giving with the passing of the ages new significance to ancient words, but never faltering in its orientation toward God,"
(*Worship,* Evelyn Underhill, Harper and Brothers, 1937, p. 215).

Women like Evelyn Underhill who become devout seekers after God's truth remind us that God gives great favors to those who truly serve him.

Section III
The Foolish Ones

"Wisdom is a fountain of life to him who has it,
but folly is the chastisement of fools" (Prov. 16:22, RSV).

The conflict between good and evil was born in the Genesis story of creation when God gave man and woman the choice between good and evil. The battle between the two continues through the saviorhood of Jesus Christ, "who gave himself for our sins to deliver us from the present evil age" (Gal. 1:4). Evil is thus of equal power with good, but the Bible teaches that good will ultimately triumph through the infinite patience of God, who shows us how to mature into holiness.

Christ is our example of the sinless life, but he pitied and had compassion upon the sinful and those sick of body. His experiences with sinners teach us that if we lived only in the company of saints we might soon feel unworthy to be about our Master's business.

Had the stories about evil and foolish human beings been entirely deleted from the Bible, it would contain no training in wisdom nor "any teaching for reproof or correction," as Paul wrote to Timothy. The early New Testament church was obviously not a sin-free congregation. Had it been, Paul's letters to them would have been only congratulatory notes instead of scathing denunciations, as they sometimes were.

Chapter 18

A Run-Away Daughter:
Dinah

(Gen. 30:21, 34:1–30)

The impulsive, indiscreet Dinah grieved her father, Jacob, and her mother, Leah, and she incensed her brothers when she showed the bad judgment to run away from her well-ordered home in the beautiful Shechem Valley. Without forewarning her family, she walked alone to the nearby town of Shechem. The prince of the town, Shechem, "the most honored of all his family," became so enamored with Dinah, that he "seized her, lay with her and humbled her."

When Jacob heard of this, he went to confer with Hamor, Shechem's father, who begged that Dinah be given to his son in marriage. But Dinah's brothers were so enraged that their sister had been treated as a common harlot that they would not agree to any kind of settlement, even after Shechem confessed his love for Dinah and begged that she become his wife.

Two hot-headed brothers, Simeon and Levi, first killed all the males in Shechem, including the young prince and his father. Then they took Dinah out of Shechem's house and probably back home with them. Afterward they took out the town's flocks, herds, and house furnishings. Finally they captured the wives and children of the men they had killed, all because of Shechem's treatment of their sister.

On his deathbed Jacob could not forgive his sons for their godlessness and treachery that brought more unhappiness to more people than the defilement of his only daughter.

Although Dinah's misdemeanor was not as serious as that of her brothers, it lighted a fire that burned everything around it.

In Dinah's experience is a lesson for young girls today who run away from home and play with fire. These words from the apocrypha apply to daughters like Dinah and point up the need for concern on the part of good fathers like Jacob.

"A daughter is a secret anxiety to her father,
and the worry of her keeps him awake at night;
when she is young, for fear she may grow too old to marry,
and when she is married, for fear she may lose her husband's
    love;
when she is a virgin, for fear she may be seduced
and become pregnant in her father's house,
when she has a husband, for fear she may misbehave,
and after marriage, for fear she may be barren.
Keep close watch over a headstrong daughter,
or she may give your enemies cause to gloat,
making you the talk of the town and a byword among the people,
and shaming you in the eyes of the world" (Ecclesiasticus 42:9–11
NEB).

Chapter 19

A Chafing Yoke:
Potiphar's Wife

(Gen. 39)

> "A bad wife is a chafing yoke;
>   controlling her is like clutching a scorpion"
> (Ecclesiasticus 26:7 NEB).

Potiphar, the captain of the Egyptian king's bodyguard, had bought Joseph, the youngest and favored son of Jacob, in the Egyptian slave market, where his brothers had sold him. When Joseph proved trustworthy, Potiphar turned over his crops, his flocks, and other business to Joseph. Everything flourished, so Potiphar felt at ease when he had to be away from home.

But Potiphar's wife was a foolish woman. Once while her husband was away on business, she tried to tempt the young Joseph, "Come and lie down with me on my couch," she pleaded.

Joseph flatly refused. "My master trusts me. How can I do such a wicked thing as this?" he asked. "It would be a great sin against God."

Joseph continued to refuse her entreaties. Outraged she grabbed his jacket and screamed. When the other servants came running to her, she told them, "See, he (my husband) has brought among us a Hebrew to insult us; he came in to me to lie with me, and I cried out with a loud voice; and when he heard that I lifted up my voice and cried, he left his garment with me, and got out of the house and fled (Gen. 39: 14, 15).

When Potiphar returned, his wife brought out Joseph's jacket and repeated the lie she had told to her servants. Naturally, Potiphar was furious at Joseph, whom he had entrusted with all he had, even his wife; so he threw Joseph into prison, where he was kept in chains.

After Joseph was released from prison, he walked to greatness, first as the prime minister of Egypt and then as the redeemer of his family, whom he brought into Egypt during a famine in Israel. Even the pharaoh recognized that Joseph was filled with the spirit of God.

Potiphar's wife disappears from the narrative as suddenly as she came. What happens to women like her, who cry out hysterically when they do not get their own way? Though rich and pampered, Potiphar's wife was actually a slave to her own immorality. Many people go through life never realizing they fool no one but themselves. Today's prototypes of Potiphar's wife never seem to understand that wisdom is enshrined in the hearts of those with common sense, but that it must shout loudly before fools will hear it. In the Book of Proverbs the foolish woman is described as noisy, wanton and knowing no shame (9:13). The foolish woman lives in a desert of her own depravity; the gracious, wise woman gains honor even into old age.

> "The way of the wicked is like deep darkness;
> they do not know over what they stumble" (Prov. 4:19).

In moments of uncertainty about how to conduct ourselves, this admonition will never fail:

> "I, wisdom, dwell in prudence,
> and I find knowledge and discretion" (Prov. 8:12)

Chapter 20

Family Difficulties:
Michal

(1 Sam. 18:8–29, 19:11–17; 2 Sam 3:13–14, 6:12–23; 1 Chron: 15:29)

King David's first wife, Michal, was born into a family that lived in constant turmoil. Her father, King Saul, was a handsome, powerful man, whose hatred and jealousy of others—especially the young, talented David—often triggered family conflict.

David was such a brilliant warrior that King Saul feared his power and finally determined to destroy him. Saul's jealousy of David intensified when he heard women choristers singing, "Saul has slain his thousands, and David his ten thousands."

One day, while David was playing his lyre for the palace guests, Saul threw his spear at David. Fortunately, David was not injured. Because the Lord seemed to be with David in every crisis and because the people loved and respected him, Saul decided to offer his older daughter Merab to David as a wife. In making this unexpected gesture, for once Saul was polite to David. "Only be valiant for me and fight the Lord's battles," he said to David.

"Who am I, and who are my kinsfolk that I should be son-in-law to the king?" David asked, for indeed he was from a family of shepherds.

But the changeable Saul went back on his promise to give Merab in marriage to David. However, his younger daughter, Michal, "really loved David." This seemed to please Saul, but when he made the offer David again asked, "Does it seem a little thing to you that I am a poor man?" Nevertheless, Michal became David's wife.

Conflicts between Saul and David multiplied, and Jonathan finally warned David that his father sought to kill him. Again as David was playing the lyre, Saul sought to pin David to the wall with a spear. Again David eluded Saul, escaped and fled. However Michal and David were soon married.

That night Michal, fearing for David's life, let him down through a window, and he fled. She then placed in their bed an effigy of David and covered it with a pillow of goat's hair. When Saul sent messengers to take David, the bed and the effigy were sent to her father.

In order to free himself from his angry father-in-law, David hid as an outlaw in exile. In the meantime to defeat David's marriage to Michal, Saul arranged another marriage for her. These were polygamous times, and David also took other wives, but when he gained full power as king over Israel, following Saul's death, David demanded that Michal be returned to him at the palace. And she was.

Sometime later, during a religious festival, Michal looked down from her window and saw David dancing and prancing in the street before the Ark of the Lord. He was dressed not in kingly attire but in a priestly ephod, probably very short and worn over his breastplate. Michal despised David in her heart when she saw how immodest he could be.

Not at all religious herself, Michal did not understand either David's religious fervor or his triumphal rituals, one of which was to come by and bless his own household, including his wife and her maids. Michal was disgusted and angered rather than pleased, and she shouted at David, "The king of Israel dishonored himself today, when he acted like a vulgar fellow before all of us."

David tried to explain, "It was before the Lord, not the maids, and the Lord made me prince over Israel. This was my way of expressing gratitude to the Lord. I may make myself more foolish than this, but whatever I do out of religious fervor will be held in honor by the maids! If they love God enough they will understand the reason for my fervor."

The Bible records nothing more about Michal, except that she died without ever bearing a child.

In the New Testament James compared an unbridled tongue, such as Michal had, to a small fire that could set ablaze a great forest. He said, "Sometimes the tongue breaks out into curses against those who are made like God." James warned against curses that come from the same mouth that also blesses others. A sharp tongue, he declared, can bring forth a poison in every part of the body until it turns its victim into a blazing flame of destruction and disaster.

The wise writer of Proverbs said that "he who keeps his mouth and his tongue keeps himself out of trouble" (21:23).

Michal's sharp tongue set in motion the sudden end of what had been a good marriage. Michal was the real loser. She lost a good home, a husband, who became Israel's greatest king, and the love of the people over whom her husband ruled.

The cause of many broken homes today may be traced to situations like those in the home of Michal and David. Most conflicts arise from the same causes—high tempers, impatience, hate, jealousy, and even sharp tongues. Homes can actually be set on fire by an unbridled tongue, especially if the tempestuous person thinks it is clever to speak his or her mind in a family crisis. The Bible teaches that the person wise enough to hold his or her tongue, is the victor. By so doing he or she may save the family in a crisis. Patience and kindness will pay dividends in the long run.

> "A soft answer turns away wrath,
>   but a harsh word stirs up anger.
> The tongue of the wise dispenses knowledge,
>   but the mouths of fools pour out folly" (Prov. 15:1–2).

Chapter 21

Deception:
Delilah

(Judg. 16)

"Please tell me Samson, why you are so strong," pleaded Delilah, a Philistine prostitute-spy. Little did Samson dream that the five war lords of the Philistines had promised Delilah a large sum to help them destroy Samson, one of Israel's tribal heroes and its strongest man physically.

Many rustic folk tales had been told about the indomitable Samson; so the Philistines set out to break his spirit and his faith in God in any way they could. They thought this would be easy, for Samson was morally weak with women.

They had probably heard that one day Samson went to the Philistine city of Gaza and spent the night with a prostitute. When the Philistines learned that Samson was vulnerable, they set a trap to destroy him through Delilah. When she first asked Samson the source of his strength, he jokingly explained that if he were tied with seven raw-leather bowstrings he might succumb. While he slept, she called the men hiding in the next room to help her tie Samson securely; but when he awoke, he "snapped the bowstrings like cotton thread."

Delilah persisted, and Samson finally told her, "If I am tied with heavy new ropes, I would be as weak as anyone else." (Judg. 16:7, The Living Bible). Samson and Delilah made love once more. Again, while Samson slept, Delilah called the men in hiding to help her tie the ropes around Samson. This time when Samson awoke, he tore loose from the ropes as if they were threads.

A third time Delilah begged Samson to tell her his secret. He suggested she weave his hair in the well of a loom and make it tight with the pin. "Then I will become weak like other men," he said. As Samson slept, Delilah gently wove his hair securely into the loom; but when he awoke, he yanked his hair from the loom.

Day after day Delilah begged Samson to tell her how he could lose his strength. At last he admitted, "A razor has never come upon my head. From birth I have been a Nazirite" (a religious devotee who has taken strict vows to God). "If my head is shaved, my strength will leave me. (A man-made tool will cut away God given strength)."

Once more Delilah lulled Samson to sleep while his head rested upon her lap. Then she called a man and had him cut off Samson's hair and shave his head. No longer could he shake himself free, for he had lost the symbol of his relationship to God, the source of his strength.

The Philistines easily captured Samson, gouged out his eyes, and took him to Gaza, where he was bound with bronze chains. As his hair began to grow again, his enemies planned a festival in the temple of their god Dagon. Samson was brought from the prison to the temple, where he stood between two pillars supporting the roof. With his great strength he brought down the walls of the temple and met death along with his captors. Delilah was probably there too.

The final tragic note about Samson is that his brothers and all his family buried him in the tomb of Manoah, his devout father.

Modern Delilahs are still playing the role of prostitute-spies, trying to trap influential men. A banker went abroad. While out to dinner with a blind date, he left his briefcase in a trusted friend's apartment. During his absence, a paid informant used the apartment key provided by the decoy-date and took the man's briefcase to the nearby home of a government informant. There its contents were photographed. It was later learned that the man's date was involved with organized crime in the country where he was a guest.

Like Samson this man learned all too late of the deception of his blind date. His reputation and his career were in shambles.

The head of an important committee in Washington was destroyed by a mischievous Delilah who caught him in a moment of weakness, when he was exhausted from overwork and too much drinking.

Another seductive woman destroyed a powerful man by revealing openly that he had had an illicit love affair with her, during which he divulged confidential government secrets that she in turn sold to his enemies.

A congressman was found to have a mistress on his payroll. He was stripped of his position and all the honors that went with it.

The Book Proverbs has this to say about the invitation of a foolish woman:

> "She sits at the door of her house,
>   she takes a seat on the high places of the town,
> calling to those who pass by,
>   who are going straight on their way,
> 'Whoever is simple, let him turn in here! . . .
> Stolen water is sweet,
>   and bread eaten in secret is pleasant.'
> But he does not know that the dead are there,
>   that her guests are in the depths of Sheol [hell]" (Prov. 9:14–18).

Chapter 22

Possessions:
Solomon's Wives

(1 Kings 3:1, 7:8–9; 11:1–8)

"Do not lay up for yourselves treasures on earth, where moth and rust consume and where thieves break in and steal, but lay up for yourselves treasures in heaven, where neither moth nor rust consumes and where thieves do not break in and steal. For where your treasure is, there will your heart be also" (Matt. 6:19).

Solomon built the first palace wing in his court in Jerusalem to honor the pharaoh's daughter, his first wife. He later built larger quarters as he took other wives, seven hundred in all from all over the ancient world, largely for political purposes to enlarge his kingdom. Each princess brought a dowry to Solomon's already flourishing empire.

When he drew up a marriage contract with the pharaoh for his daughter, she brought him rights to the Canaanite city of Gezer, which guarded one of the few passes from Jaffa to Jerusalem. In exchange for such a liberal dowry, King Solomon could afford to build her elaborate quarters. It is thought that Gezer was an ancient occupation site covering a small acreage above the Maritime Plain, guarding one of the few passes from Jafa to Jerusalem. It was afterward used by Solomon for his chariot city.

The Bible gives a detailed description of Solomon's magnificent court buildings constructed of huge stones, cut to measure, and cedars brought over mountain passes from Lebanon. These elaborate structures were trimmed with bronze, silver, and pure gold. Courts, fountains, orchards, and extensive gardens surrounded the palace. Proud peacocks, as they spread their feathers, vied in color with the court flowers and blooming fruit trees. In the court also were huge tanks shaped like goblets and movable stands of molten bronze, all decorated by skilled carvers, who decorated them with ornamental cherubims, lions, and palm trees.

Although Solomon's many wives lived among the ancient world's greatest splendor, their possessions represented only "vanity and a striving after wind." The false idols that they brought with them—Solomon sometimes stooped to worship them too—have vanished just as have their luxurious surroundings.

After Solomon's heart turned from God, adversaries rose up against him, and his large empire began to crumble. He had flagrantly violated one of the great laws handed down to Moses: "And he shall not multiply wives for himself, lest his heart turn away; nor shall he greatly multiply for himself silver and gold" (Num. 17:17).

Are we possessed by our possessions? Can the possession ever be as exciting as the pursuit? Do we forget that we came into the world with nothing and that we go out with nothing? Jesus carried nothing when he mounted the cross. Only with him can we mount the ladder of the spirit, which climbs to peace that passes understanding.

It is paradoxical that the many wives of Solomon are remembered by their possessions; the material possessions of the noblest women of the Bible are never mentioned. Deborah, for example, is remembered for her courage and valor. She counseled the people, not from a palace, but from under a tree. Hannah, the mother of Samuel, is remembered for her nobility as a mother, not by what she wore or the furnishings of her house. Although the master artists have clothed Mary, the mother of Christ, in the finest brocades and jewels, she never wore them; she was an humble peasant girl. Dorcas gave not of what she had, which was probably very little, but of herself, in "good works and acts of charity."

Solomon's worldly wives, their furnishings, their clothing, and their silver, gold, and jewels remind us that temporal possessions are worthwhile only as we make good use of them. They are never ours for long, and they can vanish quickly, even when we feel secure because of them. Without a guiding principle, life is nothing. Possessions, honors, and economic security lose their attraction when life's purpose is gone.

Faith, hope, love—and add to these wisdom—are among our greatest treasures, for they are the soul that exists in and out of time.

> "Take my instruction instead of silver,
>   and knowledge rather than choice gold;
> for wisdom is better than jewels,
>   and all that you may desire cannot compare with her. . . .
> My fruit is better than gold, even fine gold,
>   and my yield than choice silver.
> I walk in the way of righteousness,
>   in the paths of justice,
> endowing with wealth those who love me,
>   and filling their treasuries" (Prov. 8:10–11, 19–21).

Chapter 23

A Battle with Evil:
The Three Who Denounce God

Jezebel, 1 Kings 16:31; 18:4, 13, 19, 19:1–2; 21:5, 7, 11, 14, 15, 23, 25;
II Kings 9:7, 10, 29, 30, 32–37;
Athaliah, II Kings 8:26; 11:1–3, 13–14, 20;
II Chron. 22:2, 10–12; 23:12–13, 21: 24:7;
Herodias, Matt. 14:3, 6; Mark 15:17, 19, 22 Luke 3:19

"Fools, when will you be wise?" (Pss. 94:8).

The lives of Jezebel and her daughter Athaliah speak loudly about fools who perish for want of wisdom.

"Take him out and stone him to death," ordered Jezebel, wife of King Ahab, second in the dynasty reigning at Samaria, when their neighbor Naboth refused to release to them part of his vineyard.

After Naboth was stoned to death, Jezebel commanded, "Take possession of the vineyard of Naboth, which he has refused to give you for money; for he is not alive but dead."

These vicious commands are enough to identify Jezebel, a princess of the Sidonians, worshipers of Baal. She hated the one God of Israel and ordered her husband, King Ahab, to kill the prophets of the Lord. She fought a continuing battle with the noblest of them all, the great Elijah, who finally fled from her persecution after she had warned him, "So may the gods do to me, and more also, if I do not make your life as miserable as any one of them by this time tomorrow." She did just that. A drouth predicted by Elijah forced him to flee to the brook of Cherith, east of the Jordan, and on to Zarephath.

Jezebel was evil to the core. She fed at her own table the prophets of the false gods of her idolatrous cult of Baal. The people hated these prophets because they tried to destroy belief in the God of righteousness, law, and order.

Jezebel exercised such an evil power over her husband that it is written, "Ahab did more to provoke the Lord, the God of Israel to anger than all the kings of Israel who were before him" (I Kings 16:33).

Finally she was thrown from her own palace window, where she sat in regal attire, defying her enemies. Her blood was "spattered on the wall of her ivory palace and on the horses as they trampled over her."

Jezebel engendered wickedness in her family. Her daughter Athaliah, her sons, King Ahaziah and King Jehoram, as well as her grandchildren. Athaliah, like her mother, instigated horrible court murders in order to achieve power. At the end of Athaliah's short reign over the southern kingdom of Judah, wickedness was all across her path. Athaliah promoted Baal worship and actuated murders that shocked the people. She was probably behind the murders of the brothers of her husband, another King Jehoram, because they were still loyal to the northern kingdom of Israel, where her father, Ahab, was king and her mother, Jezebel, the queen consort.

Athaliah's husband died young, and she stepped down as queen-mother when her son, another Ahaziah, came to the throne. Soon he had the priests of the Lord murdered. Athaliah was probably behind this evil also, for the Bible reports that she was "her son's counsellor in wickedness."

When her son died young of an incurable disease, Athaliah seized the throne again and had all the royal blood relations, even her grandchildren, murdered. Only one of the royal infants was rescued. This was Joash by her stepdaughter. As Athaliah, who had ruled Judah for six years, heard the people celebrating this boy-king's ascension to the throne, she screamed "Treason, treason." Afterward she was slain at the palace gates. The horses trampled over her dead body, and neither family nor friends mourned her death.

Herodias, wife of Herod Antipas, tetrarch of Galilee and Peraea, initiated the beheading of John the Baptist, the cousin of Jesus Christ.

John had denounced her incestuous marriage to Herod Antipas, tetrarch of Galilee and Peraea and brother of her first husband, Herod Philip, from whom she was divorced after she persuaded Herod Antipas to divorce his wife. In the presence of King Herod's banqueting guests, she requested, through her dancing daughter, that the head of John the Baptist be brought to her on a silver platter.

The lives of these godless women remind us of the words of Proverbs 11.

"The crookedness of the treacherous [like Jezebel and Athaliah] destroys them" (Prov. 11:3).

The godless man (or woman like Herodias) perish in their own wickedness. The unrighteous fall by their own plots and plans.

A false balance [of the wicked of evil over good] is an abomination to the Lord" (Prov. 11:1).

In wisdom "there is a spirit intelligent and holy, unique . . . . subtle, free-moving , . . . all-powerful , . . . and permeating all intelligent, pure, and delicate spirits. . . . Wisdom moves more easily than motion itself, she pervades and permeates all things because she is so pure. Like a fine mist she rises from the power of God, the pure effluence from the glory of the Almighty; . . . She is the brightness that streams from everlasting light, the flawless mirror of the active power of God and the image of his goodness" (Wisd. of Sol. 7:22–26, NEB).

Although the ungodly may prosper for a time, their hope "is like down flying in the wind, like spindrift swept before a storm and smoke which the wind whirls away" (Wisd. of Sol. 5:14, NAB).

Section IV
The Understanding Hearts

"A word fitly spoken
is like apples of gold in a setting of silver" (Prov. 25:11).

Wise women know that spoken words are powerful and that truth is adorned with beauty. Abigail was wise when she went before the young David to express, not only appreciation for his kindness, but also her keen insight into David's nature and her unfaltering assurance that he was a man of destiny. After the death of Abigail's husband, David remembered that Abigail was a wise woman, and he sent for her to become his wife.

The wise woman of Abel displayed great understanding in her analysis of an impending disaster to her city. She told David's commander that if his men were permitted to destroy her city they would "swallow up the heritage of the Lord."

The real mother of an illegitimate son revealed wisdom and love when she went before King Solomon to save the life of her son. Another mother who lived with the real mother also claimed the child. Because the two mothers could not agree on to whom the child belonged, King Solomon asked that his sword be brought to him to slay the child.

Spoke the real mother, "O, my Lord, give her the living child and by no means slay it." Her sagacity was almost equal to that of Solomon.

Others in this section are the Queen of Sheba, whose search for wisdom has been extolled since Bible times, and Queen Esther, who left a record of wisdom for her people.

Chapter 24

A Quiet Strength:
Abigail

(1 Sam. 25:1–42)

Abigail, the beautiful woman of "good understanding," suffered an ill-matched first marriage. Her husband, Nabal, drank heavily. When he was drunk, no one, not even Abigail, could converse with him.

The young David and his men voluntarily watched over Nabal's three thousand sheep and one thousand goats. David had accepted nothing from Nabal for his service. Then one day when Nabal was celebrating a feast at his home and David learned that his young sheepherders were hungry, he sent some of his men to ask for food.

"Who is David?" railed the drunken Nabal. "There are many servants today who are breaking away from their masters."

No one could have been more discourteous or less informed. David was a well-known sheepherder who had befriended Nabal, and David was his own master.

When the wise Abigail learned about her husband's rude behavior, she hastily prepared food for David and his men, who were camped in the wilderness nearby. She and her servants mounted asses and loaded them with large quantities of bread, wine, dressed sheep, parched grain, raisins, and figs.

Abigail's first words to David were typical of a humble, worthy woman. "Upon me alone, my Lord, be the guilt," she said. "Do not be offended by my ill-natured husband, for folly is with him.

Please forgive my trespassing in bringing you food to make amends for him."

Her next words were prophetic. "The Lord be with you, for you are fighting his battles. If men rise up to pursue you and to seek your life, the Lord will protect you. And when he has done to you according to all the good he has promised, you shall have no cause for grief or regret for having to shed blood."

As David bade Abigail goodbye, he said, "Blessed be the Lord, the God of Israel, who sent you this day to meet me! Blessed be your discretion, and blessed be you, who have kept me this day from bloodguilt" (1 Sam. 25:32-33).

Both Abigail and David acted promptly, discretely, and effectively in a difficult situation. Each was willing to make and accept apology, and each revealed a belief in God's goodness to right a difficult situation. The forbearance, prudence, kindness, and diplomacy that Abigail and David showed for each other averted a tragedy.

Nabal was sick, irritable, and unreasonable when Abigail returned home. He was "very drunk." The discerning Abigail told Nabal nothing until morning. This time the churlish Nabal turned cold as stone toward Abigail; yet it was she who had saved his life and his house. About ten days later Nabal died, the victim of his own intemperance and anger.

The respected Abigail was highly honored after Nabal's death. David had seen that she was a woman of good understanding; so he sent his servants saying he wanted her to be his wife.

"She rose and bowed with her face to the ground, and said, 'Behold, your handmaid is a servant to wash the feet of the servants of my lord.' And Abigail made haste and rose and mounted on an ass, and her five maidens attended her; she went after the messengers of David, and became his wife" (1 Sam. 25:41–42).

She, who had once lived in such uncertainty, now fulfilled her destiny as wife of King David and the mother of one son Chilead. She is Honored as one of the wisest women in the days of the kings of Israel and as one of the best known and best loved of King David's eight wives. Abigail's love of God and her womanly wisdom, not only saved her from disaster, but brought joy and romance to her later.

Her experience is a good example of how to deal with a spouse who has a serious drinking problem, about which the Book of Proverbs does not mince words:

> "At last it [drinking] bites like a serpent,
>   and stings like an adder.
> Your eyes will see strange things,
>   and your mind utter perverse things" (Prov. 23:32–33).

There is also this other wise counsel in Proverbs that applies to Abigail and others like her:

> "Make wisdom too your own;
> if you find it, you may look forward to the future,
> and your thread of life will not be cut short" (Prov. 24:14, NEB).

Chapter 25

A Public Servant:
The Wise Woman of Abel

(2 Sam. 20:16–22)

This woman of the town of Abel is usually identified in most translations as the "wise woman," She was wise indeed in her analysis of the impending destruction of her city, in her willingness to talk to David's powerful commander-in-chief Joab, and in her vision.

"I am one of those who are peaceable and faithful in Israel; you seek to destroy a city which is a mother in Israel; why will you swallow up the heritage of the Lord?" she asked Joab.

He answered, "I have no desire to destroy your city, but you have one man, Sheba, who has lifted up his hand against King David. Give him up, and I will withdraw from the city."

This woman assured Joab that Sheba's head would be thrown to him over the wall.

That is a strong declaration for a so-called wise woman, but these were ancient times. The impending disaster to an entire city and all its people would be a far greater loss than the death of one man.

Wisdom is defined as the knowledge of what is true or right and the willingness to act justly. In her wisdom this woman knew she had to take drastic action. First, it would save the lives of hundreds of her townspeople and their property. Second, the people would be free again. Their pride would be renewed too in a place recognized as "the heritage of the Lord."

Abel must have been a place of beauty. Several biblical towns are called Abel, and the name has many picturesque meanings.

It signifies "a meadow of vineyards," "a dance place by a perennial stream," "a city of acacia trees," and "a watercourse of vineyards." The exact location of this particular Abel is unknown, but the people's love for their town suggests it was a place worth saving.

This woman was wise enough to know that such God-given beauty must not be destroyed in a day's time by invaders, all because of one evil man. She was prudent and understanding, and she combined knowledge with love for her town. Her wisdom served as a safeguard in time of impending destruction and demonstrates that wisdom is more to be valued than physical beauty in a person's life and that it is a more effective weapon than war.

> "Wisdom raises her sons (and daughters) to greatness
> and cares for those who seek her.
> To love her is to love life:
> to rise early for her sake is to be filled with joy" (Ecclesiasticus
> 4:11-12, NEB).

Chapter 26

The Love
of the Real Mother:
Two Prostitutes with Sons

(1 Kings 3:16–28; Prov. 12:16–18)

Two mothers, described as prostitutes sharing the same living quarters, argued over the fate of their two newborn sons, born three days apart. Now one lay dead.

The first mother declared that the living son was hers. The other mother said, "No, the living son is mine."

While no witnesses were around, these mothers had given birth to sons. One child died in the night when one of the mothers lay over it while she was sleeping. The first mother was sure she knew her own child, the one who was alive and well, but the second mother claimed this child. So the two mothers went to King Solomon.

In explaining her dilemma, the first mother said, "She [the mother who lay on her son in her sleep] arose at midnight, and took my son beside me, while . . . [I] slept, and laid it in her bosom, and laid her dead son in my bosom. When I rose in the morning to nurse my child, behold, it was dead, but when I looked at it closely . . . , it was not the child that I had borne" (1 Kings 3:20–21).

The second mother told a different story: "The living child is mine, and the dead child is hers."

But the other rebutted, "No, the dead child is yours, and the living child is mine."

The argument went on while King Solomon listened intently. The second mother exclaimed loudly again, "This is my son that is alive, and your son is dead."

The first one came right back and said, "No, but your son is dead and my son is the living one."

King Solomon, then in the peak years of his wisdom, prayed for an understanding heart to discern between good and bad. Finally he spoke the fatal words: "Bring me a sword. Divide the living child in two, and give half to the one, and half to the other."

The first mother whose son was alive, sighed, "Oh, my lord, give her the living child, and by no means slay it."

The mother of the dead son, exclaimed loudly, "It shall be neither mine nor yours, divide it."

But the real mother, through her great love for her child, said, "Oh, my lord, give her the living child, and by no means slay it."

King Solomon, now certain of the real mother, judged wisely: said, "Give the living child to the first woman, and by no means slay it. She is its mother."

All Israel perceived that King Solomon possessed the wisdom of God to render justice. The real mother was also wise in the calm way she handled the situation. Her own last remark, "by no means slay the child," was his guide in rendering justice. She had real love for her child, and this love guided her. She could not go wrong. With love in her heart and justice in King Solomon's heart, there could be no injustice.

The Book of Proverbs was probably compiled by a group of writers during King Solomon's reign. It delineates the character of these two mothers without even mentioning their case.

> "The vexation of a fool is known at once,
>   but the prudent man (or woman) ignores an insult.
> He [or she] who speaks the truth gives honest evidence,
>   but a false witness utters deceit.
> There is one whose rash words are like sword thrusts,
>   but the tongue of the wise brings healing.
> Truthful lips endure for ever,
>   but a lying tongue is but for a moment" (Prov. 12:16–19).

Chapter 27

In Search of Wisdom:
The Queen of Sheba

(1 Kings 10:1–10; 2 chron. 9:1–12; Matt. 12:42; Luke 11:31, Eccles. 43:15–33)

"The report was true which I heard in my own land of your affairs and of your wisdom, but I did not believe the reports until I came and my own eyes had seen it; . . . the half was not told me; your wisdom and prosperity surpass the report, which I heard" (1 Kings 10:6–7). Thus spoke the Queen of Sheba when she, along with her retinue—camels bearing spices, much gold, and precious stones—arrived in Jerusalem to visit King Solomon and his court. She traveled by caravan from Saba in southwestern Arabia, not only to bear gifts, but to ask questions.

She was a remarkable woman for these ancient times. Saba honored its women and acknowledged them as equal to men. They were granted the same civil, religious, and military rights. King Solomon was impressed with this great lady from afar and was flattered by her diplomatic remarks: "Happy are your wives! Happy are these your servants, who continually stand before you and hear your wisdom! Blessed be the Lord your God, who has delighted in you and set you on the throne of Israel! Because the Lord loved Israel for ever, he has made you king, that you may execute justice and righteousness" (1 Kings 10:8–9).

The Queen of Sheba not only heaped praise upon King Solomon but also the most lavish gifts obtainable—120 talents of gold and large quantities of spices and precious stones. In turn King Solomon gave her many gifts. This was during Israel's greatest commercial expansion, and the Queen of Sheba was prompted to work out a trade alliance with King Solomon. Later

he and King Hiram of Tyre sent a joint merchant fleet to pro-
cure luxuries from Saba and more distant countries.

This queen from the south, as Jesus later called her, was so
impressed with the House of Lebanon that Solomon had built,
"the food of his table, the seating of his officials, and the attend-
ance of his servants, their clothing, his cupbearers, and his burnt
offerings which he offered at the house of the Lord" (1 Kings
10:5) that she returned home more inspired with what she had
seen with her own eyes than what she had heard from afar.

Nine centuries later, when Jesus began his ministry, the
people were still familiar with the story of the wisdom and power
of Solomon and the acclaimed glory of the queen of Sheba.
When the Pharisees came before Jesus seeking proof of his
teachings, he told them about something infinitely more important than the wisdom and wealth of Solomon, which had gone
when he lost sight of God and when he began to worship at
pagan shrines with his foreign wives. Amid such wondrous
things as Jesus taught, the glories of Solomon faded into insig-
nificance, as if they had never existed.

That something greater was light (the presence of God) and
truth (the reality of the universe of God) and Faith that ac-
knowledges the existence and power of a supreme being and the
reality of a divine order.

What do we search for most today? Where does that search
end? In equal rights? In vocational success? In worldly pleasures? Or do we search for the knowledge to make the right choices
about those things that are lasting and good? Are we looking so
hard for signs of man-made wonders that we are blind to God's
wonders?

Where can we find the skill to praise God for his creation? In
the clear vault of the sky, the sun coming into view as it rises, the
moon, a perpetual sign to mark the divisions of time, brilliant
stars that light the sky, a rainbow that rounds the sky with its
gleaming arc, or clouds that fly out like birds.

The writer of Ecclesiasticus said that there is no way to
exhaust our theme of something more wondrous. We can praise
God eternally.

"Summon all your strength to declare his greatness.
and be untiring, for the most you can do will fall
short.

Has anyone ever seen him, to be able to describe him?
  Can anyone praise him as he truly is?
  We have seen but a small part of his works,
    and there remain many mysteries greater still.
      The Lord has made everything
and has given wisdom to the godly" (Ecclesiasticus
43:30–33, NEB).

Chapter 28

Queenly Self-Denial:
Esther

(Book of Esther)

Because she was chosen the most 'beautiful and lovable" among the young virgins in 127 provinces in an empire stretching from India to Ethiopia, Esther, a poor, unknown Jewish maiden, became the wife of King Ahasuerus, emperor of a vast Media-Persian empire. And she sat on the royal throne with the king in Susa, the capital.

Her foster father, Mordecai, also her cousin, inspired her to believe that she had a tremendous opportunity for good during this time when her Jewish people were being severely persecuted. Mordecai knew that all the Jews in Persia might be annihilated by Haman, the wicked prime minister and the king's favorite.

"Think not that in the king's palace you will escape any more than all the other Jews," Mordecai warned Esther. "For if you keep silence at such a time as this, relief and deliverance will rise for the Jews ... and your father's house will perish. And who knows whether you have not come to the kingdom for such time as this?" (4:13–14).

Even though the stakes were high, Esther courageously declared, "Then I will go to the king, though it is against the law; and if I perish, I perish" (4:16). First she prepared a banquet honoring the king and Haman, and in the presence of both of them, she humbly declared, "If I have found favor in your sight, O king, and if it pleases the king, let my life be given me at my petition, and my people at my request. For we are sold, I and my people, to be destroyed, . . . If we had been sold merely as slaves, . . . I would have held my peace."

Then Ahasuerus asked Esther, "Who is he, and where is he?"

And Esther answered "A foe and enemy! This wicked Haman!"

Finally, Haman was the one annihilated, and "the Jews had light and gladness and joy and honor" (8:16) again.

Queen Esther was such a catalyst for good that she seemed to have been born for "such a time as this," and she accepted the responsibility out of love for her people, even if it meant she would perish with them. In nobly accepting her destiny as protector of her people, Esther took a stand that could have meant not only the loss of her place as queen but her death. Fate was against her because Haman had offered a vast sum to the king if he would purge and destroy the Jewish people. The power of Haman vanished soon after Esther pled before the king, and Haman was hung.

Although Esther lived at a time of intense hatred and revenge, and although she is guilty of racial intolerance herself, she did save her people from annihilation.

The destruction of a culture has often been threatened in an insidious manner like the one planned by Haman. What has made the difference and kept civilization on its course is the courage of people like Esther, a woman of great spirit. Powerful though her husband was and young though she was, she encouraged him to see that he who rules must be just. In his great love for her, he conceded to her wishes.

In a sense Esther was another Deborah. She also exhibited the spirit of the early martyrs and saints, who were willing to die for what they believed right. Esther had the courage to cut away at the roots of evil; she arose to defend her people without hesitation and without thought of herself.

Even now all kinds of evils threaten our own civilization: nuclear bombs could destroy us in an instant! The resources of some countries are exhausted and thousands of people are starving; others are ruled by corrupt leaders that threaten the freedom of the entire world. But doors that open to triumph still await the courageous and the valiant.

The leadership of one capable, dedicated person like Esther can change the course of history. Her sacrifice did counteract the annihilation of all the Jews in Persia and opened wide new doors for them. The doors she went through to triumph, were first selflessness, then truth, justice, faith, and love. As she walked through these doors Esther attained an abiding, creative power well described in Alfred Tennyson's (1809-1892) verse from Aenone, personifying Aeon, an age of the universe, an immeasurable length of time.

THE WAY TO POWER

Self-reverence, self-knowledge, self-control,
These three alone lead life to sovereign power.
Yet not for power (power of herself
Would come uncall'd for) but to live by law,
Acting the law we live by without fear;
And, because right is right, to follow right
Were wisdom in the scorn of consequence.

Section V

Widowhood—A Long Journey Alone

Only the woman suddenly thrust into widowhood knows how traumatic the experience can be. It is been that way since Bible times. In this section we shall see that widowhood represents a broad spectrum of emotions: faith and fear, hope and hopelessness, kindness and unkindness, confidence and timidity, security and insecurity, love and loneliness. Also we shall see that the Bible expresses great concern for the widow and that many laws specifically protected her, such as, "You shall not afflict any widow" (Exod. 22:22). "For the Lord your God executes . . . justice for the . . . widow" (Deut. 10:17–18),

Isaiah spoke with deep feelings about widows,

> "seek justice,
> correct oppression;
> defend the fatherless,
> plead for the widow" (Isa. 1:17)

Desolation runs through the account of Ichabod's mother, the first widow delineated here. On the other hand the second chapter deals with two widows alone, Ruth and Naomi, who met hardships victoriously. The next two chapters deal first with a widow's empty cupboard, and next a hungry widow and her son who died but was raised back to life. Another chapter has as its model the widow who tossed her last two coins into the chest in the temple at Jerusalem and attracted Jesus because of her sacrifice. There is also the story of the steadfast widow in Jesus's parable. She assures all of us that "by steadfastness and by the encouragement of scriptures we might have hope" (Rom. 15:4). Finally our most blessed assurance is this,

> "Blessed be the God and Father of our Lord Jesus Christ, the Father of mercies and God of all comfort, who comforts us in all our afflictions, so that we may be able to comfort those who are in any affliction, with the comfort with which we ourselves are comforted by God. For as we share abundantly in Christ's suffering, so through Christ we share abundantly in comfort too" (2 Cor. 1:1–3).

Chapter 29

A Desolate Widow:
The Mother of Ichabod

(1 Sam. 4:19–22)

When the pregnant daughter-in-law of Eli, the priest in the Temple at Shiloh, where Hannah took Samuel, heard that her husband and his brother were dead she went into labor and gave birth to a son. She was so grief-stricken that even when the midwives told her about the child, she could only murmur, "Name the child Ichabod, for the glory has departed from Israel." And she died.

Her husband and brother were killed in battle while the Ark of the Covenant was in their care. Her ninety-year-old father-in-law died from a broken neck when he fell from a fence.

This desolate widow, who had lived amid defeat, disappointment and depression, probably had little love for and little companionship with her child's father, for it was known that he and his brother "lay with women who served at the entrance to the tent of meeting . . . and they would not listen to the voice of their father" (I Sam. 2:22, 25), who presided as priest. The disappearance of the Ark of the Covenant must have been a source of embarrassment to this desolate widow and her family.

Anxiety and hopelessness buried her beneath her sorrows. You would have thought God was dead, but God was not dead. She was only dead to his wonders and miracles. Suppose she, like Ruth and Naomi, had sought to go forward in faith, despite grief. Or suppose she had prayed for her child before birth, as Hannah did.

The pages of history are filled with stories of widows who

reared their children alone and would not accept defeat, no matter how hopeless their future appeared. Because of their strengths and their struggles they gave back to their sons and daughters a greatness that grew out of hardship. The lives and prayers of many widowed mothers are written into words like these by Bliss Carman (1861-1929), *Masterpieces of Religious Verse* (p. 298–299).

LORD OF THE FAR HORIZONS

"Lord of the far horizons,
   Give us the eyes to see
Over the verge of sundown
   The beauty that is to be.
Give us the skill to fashion
   The task of Thy command,
Eager to follow the pattern
   We may not understand.

Master of ancient wisdom
   And the lore lost long ago,
Inspire our foolish reason,
   With faith to seek and know.

When the skein of truth is tangled,
   And the lead of sense is blind,
Foster the fire to lighten
   Our illumined mind."

Chapter 30

Two Widows Alone:
Ruth and Naomi

(Book of Ruth)

Naomi is best remembered for the wise and loving arrangement she made with her daughter-in-law Ruth. Both Naomi's husband and her two sons, the husbands of Ruth and Orpha, were dead, and she wanted to leave Moab and return to her home in Bethlelem. She said to her daughters-in-law, "Go, return each of you, to your mother's house. May the Lord deal kindly with you, as you have dealt with the dead and with me. . . . May each of you marry again" (paraphrase of Ruth 1:8–9).

Then she kissed them, and the three women wept. Orpha said goodbye, but Ruth clung to Naomi, begging, "Entreat me not to leave you or to return from following you; for where you go I will go, and where you lodge I will lodge; your people shall be my people, and your God my God; where you die I will die, and there will I be buried. May the Lord do so to me and more also if even death parts me from you." And so together Ruth and Naomi journeyed to Bethlehem.

They arrived at the beginning of the barley harvest. In order to provide a living for both of them, Ruth went to work in a field as a gleaner.

"I went away full, and the Lord has brought me back empty," Naomi explained to Ruth. But the loving Ruth stayed right beside Naomi, lodging where she lodged, and accepting Naomi's people as her people, and Naomi's God as her God. When Naomi became despondent over their problems as widows,

Ruth's beautiful spirit uplifted her. When Naomi counseled with Ruth, she listened, even when Naomi directed her to go and glean in the field of Boaz, her husband's kinsman. This was wise advice. Boaz admired the modest Ruth and arranged to marry her.

Ruth and Naomi cooperated every step of the way, even after Ruth's marriage to Boaz and after Naomi went to lodge in their home. Their fondness for each other reached its fullness when a son, Obed, was born to Ruth and Boaz. This child became Naomi's child too, and the love she had for him helped to make up for the loss of her two sons and her husband.

Naomi's grandson Obed, destined to be the father of Jesse, the father of David, lifted Naomi and Ruth to glorious heights. What they had left behind in Moab seemed to be returned to them tenfold, for Boaz was a well-to-do man, as well as a kind and loving provider for his family.

The story of Ruth, who loved her mother-in-law so devotedly, and Naomi, who returned that love, is one of literature's most moving accounts of abiding love. Neither ever disappointed the other, even during severe hardships. Each sacrificed for the other, and each in turn was blessed in the happiness they found together.

Widows like Ruth and Naomi learn to thank God for the opportunity to graciously accept widowhood, a phase of life for which all women must prepare themselves. In doing so, they bring deeper meaning into this prayer by the American theologian Reinhold Niebuhr:

> O God, give us the serenity to accept what can not be changed;
>   courage to change what should be changed;
> and wisdom to distinguish one from the other.

Chapter 31

An Empty Cupboard, A Dying Son:
The Widow of Zarephath

(1 Kings 17:8–24)

   This widow, identified only by the town in which she lived, learned from the prophet Elijah how to overcome her fears. She found herself in two of the most critical situations a widow can face: an empty cupboard in the midst of a drought, and the sudden death of her only son.
   Elijah came upon her at the city gates, where she was gathering a few sticks to make a fire. He saw immediately that she was in trouble, and he understood. He had just come from the Trans-Jordan brook of Cherith, where he had lived in its tangled underbrush, an excellent hiding place for a fugitive prophet fleeing the wrath of Jezebel. There by the brook he was first fed bread and meat by the ravens, but then as the drought continued, the brook dried up. He fled to Zarephath and there came upon the widow, whom he asked for a cup of water. As she went for it, he called out, "Bring me also a morsel of bread."
   In a frightened voice, she answered, "I have nothing baked, only a handful of meal in a jar, and a little oil in a cruse; and now, I am gathering a couple of sticks, that I may go in and prepare for myself and my son, that we may eat it, and die" (1 Kings 17:12).
   After Elijah assured her that she must not be afraid, she saw the flour and oil miraculously multiply. He promised that there would be no lack for days.
   Soon after this, the woman's son died suddenly. She found Elijah and accused him: "What have you against me, O man of

God? You have come to me to bring my sin to remembrance, and to cause the death of my son!" (1 Kings 17:18).

Elijah asked her to give him her son, and when he had taken him into his arms, he prayed. The child was miraculously aroused from death, and Elijah took him to his waiting mother. "I know that you are a man of God, and that the word of the Lord in your mouth is truth," she told Elijah.

Such miracles, so inspiringly related in the Bible, do not belong to ancient times only. They are as possible now as they were then if we learn to quell our fears and to know that God is near—in drought, famine, or pestilence. This widow had to learn, as do all of us in time of fear, how to draw closer to God for help. We may never know starvation of the body, but all of us experience moments when the streams of inspiration run dry, when our material resources are diminished, when illness or death hangs over our families.

Wise is the woman who seeks to build spiritual reserves so that when sorrow and tragedy come she can meet them with courage. We require spiritual reserves at every period in our lives, but especially in widowhood. In this age of plenty, our fears are not the same as those of the poor widow of Zarephath, but we have other fears that are just as difficult to conquer. If all the blessings that come to the suffering were recorded, we would better know that God does not forsake his own today any more than he did in the time of Elijah.

Since the seventeenth century, this verse from a hymn by Paul Gerhardt (1607-1676) and translated by John Wesley (1703-1791) has inspired and renewed the distressed:

> Give to the winds your fears. Hope and be undismayed;
> God hears your sighs, and counts your tears; God shall lift
>   up your head
> Through waves and clouds and storms He gently clears the way;
> Wait your his time, so shall the night soon end in joyous day.

Chapter 32

Want and Hunger:
Widow with Two Children

(2 Kings 4:1–7)

Her cupboard was empty. A creditor had come to take her sons as slaves for debts she could not pay. She would be alone, denied their love, and still in great want herself.

This widow's needs were not unlike those of the widow of Zarephath. Elisha, a prophet of mercy, now carried on in Elijah's footsteps, and this widow felt free to call upon Elisha for help. Part of his ministry was to the widows and orphans of a religious order, the sons of the prophets, of whom her husband was one.

"My husband is dead," she told Elisha. "You know that I feared the Lord, but the creditor has come for my children." Elisha's first question was "What have you in the house?"

She said, "I have nothing in the house, except a jar of oil."

Then he told her, "Go outside, borrow vessels of all your neighbors, empty the vessels, as many as you can find. Then go in, and shut the door upon yourself and your sons, and pour oil into all those vessels. When one is full, set it aside" (paraphrase of 2 Kings 4:3–4).

The widow left Elisha and shut the door upon herself and her sons, who brought the vessels to her. When the oil was miraculously multiplied and the vessels full, she said, "Bring me another vessel."

"There is not another," the sons said. Then the oil stopped flowing. There was no need for more.

When she told this to Elisha, he said, "Go, sell the oil and pay your debts, and you and your sons can live on the rest."

Oil, usually olive oil, was a necessity to the homemaker in these times. It was used for currency as well as for anointing. On the table, it took the place of butter, and it was mixed with meat and meal. It also gave light in the house and was used for medicinal purposes. One good olive tree would yield ten or fifteen gallons of oil in each year of plenty, but this was a time of drought so there was no oil. The homemaker without oil was in dire need.

This widow came to the right person. Elisha was a man of wonder who cared about the needs of others. His far-reaching ministry took him from Bethel to Jericho to Dothan to Gilgal. She probably knew he had learned how to suspend the laws of nature, how to predict the future, and most of all how to sense the needs of others and do something about them.

We can not explain how the oil multiplied any more than we can explain how the sun, moon and the stars remain suspended in the firmament. But Elisha, a man of God, knew the mystery of many of God's miracles, and he used his knowledge to help others. He exemplified the meaning of Psalm 23:

"The Lord is my shepherd, I shall not want;
　　he makes me to lie down in green pastures.
He leads me beside still waters;
　　he restores my soul,
He leads in paths of righteousness
　　for his name's sake.

Even though I walk through the valley of the shadow of death,
　　I fear no evil:
for thou art with me:
　　thy rod and thy staff,
　　they comfort me.

Thou preparest a table before me
　　in the presence of my enemies;
thou anointest my head with oil,
　　my cup overflows.
Surely goodness and mercy shall follow me
　　all the day of my life;
and I shall dwell in the house of the Lord
　　for ever."

This widow's oil overflowed until there was such plenty she

needed no more. Her debts were paid with the surplus, and her children were not taken into slavery. She knew what it was to realize that goodness and mercy would follow her all the days of her life.

Miracles are all about us today, although we sometimes fail to recognize them. What of the light that shines in the darkness? What of the dreams that come true? What of the oil well that gushes in on desert land? What of these and countless other expressions of the statement that "the earth is the Lord's and the fullness thereof?" Why should we ever fear?

We can learn to reach into the invisible presence of the creative spirit God, with whom nothing is impossible, for he controls and determines all things. When we attain this knowledge, there is plenty for all of our needs, greater than we ever dreamed in our time of want. If we look back in our lives, we can remember miracles not unlike those of the children of Israel when the waters of the Red Sea parted and Moses led them across, when they were fed manna and quail during their time of wandering over an empty desert, when the waters of the Jordan were parted and Joshua led them back to Canaan, home at last.

Chapter 33

The Miracle of Giving:
A Widow's Coin

(Mark 12:41–44; Luke 21:1–4)

A poor widow with two copper coins (a penny) is her only identification. Her two coins hardly made a tinkle as she dropped them into the coffer in the Temple at Jerusalem. Unlike the scribes, "who like to wear long robes, . . . occupy the best seats in the market place. . . . who devour widows' houses and for a pretense make long prayers" (Mark 12:38–40, RSV), this meek woman made her way quietly.

Jesus sat opposite the treasury, watching people place their coins into the collection box. The rich nonchalantly put in large sums, and the poor faithfully deposited their mites. Like the widow, most of the poor had to live by faith the rest of the week if they put in anything at all. Recognizing that this particular woman was especially poor in the world's goods but rich in her love of God, Jesus called his disciples and explained, "Truly, I say to you, this poor widow has put in more than all those who are contributing to the treasury. For they all contributed out of their abundance; but she out of her poverty has put in everything she had, her whole living" (Mark 12:43–44).

Her coins, if found below temple ruins today, would probably have unbelievable monetary value as a collector's item, but that isn't what this story is about. It is about the sacrifice of this poor widow, whose giving has inspired millions of small givers throughout history.

Thousands of women on every continent—some living in isolated villages and others in big cities—have felt the reality of her sacrifice through the Fellowship of the Least Coin. With the smallest coins of each country, often less than a penny, they give one coin at a time, twelve times annually. This unique association of hundreds of thousands of women started in Bangkok in 1956 because the Asian women were weary of "always being on the receiving end." They chose the least coin of their own country as their gift to God so that all women everywhere could stand equal before God and one another. If they had no coins, they could offer a couple of eggs or a handful of rice. The more important thing was the prayer that winged the request that God should bring peace to the world. The Asian Christian mothers confessed "when my son dies on a battlefield, a little of me dies, too."

This concern for all people everywhere has spread around the world until it now includes more than sixty nations, several of them behind the Iron Curtain. Since the gifts are so small, the receptacle could easily cost more than the coins, which the women save in different ways. In Malaya they use as piggy banks short sticks of bamboo. In India they stick their paisa (a fraction of an American penny) onto their walls with mud.

The Fellowship of the Least Coin now distributes hundreds of thousands of dollars all over the world. Some walk twenty-five miles to a church meeting to give their small coins, which have gone to fight drug addiction in the United States, to build a tiny chapel on an isolated peninsula in Japan, to help tubercular cripples in Hong Kong, and to set a rehabilitation colony for former prostitutes—many blind, feeble-minded, or paralyzed.

Probably the most meaningful contribution these worldwide Christian women make is to the least wanted children of Ceylon, the crippled or seriously retarded, for whom no one finds room. Sometimes these children are left in ashcans in dim alleys or by the roadside wrapped in newspapers.

Grace Nies Fletcher wrote about these and other such children in her book, *In Quest of the Least Coin* (William Morrow & Co., 1968). She tells of seeing "babies with heads almost as large as their bodies, spastic four-year-olds whose legs were so twisted that they were twined around their necks and could not be straightened out, babies with lack-luster eyes and gaping mouths" (p. 96).

But these children of all faiths—Buddhists, Christians, Moslems, and Hindus—through the power of small gifts and prayers, are cared for with compassion and love, and the directors leave the rest to God. Those who work with them do not always understand the mysterious power of the least coins, but like the gift of the widow with the two mites, miracles come forth. The mystery of God's work goes on through the least coins, of which Sara Lindsay writes so well in Mrs. Fletcher's book (p. 51),

> With careless hand I gave the coin,
> It seemed as nought to me.
> The least of all my goodly share
> As gift? A mockery!
>
> My sister in her distant land
> Gave one least coin, like me;
> But went without her evening bread
> To share her poverty.
>
> Within the cup which feeds Thy lambs,
> Our coins became, through Thee,
> The golden coin of Fellowship—
> Thy love—the alchemy.

In our affluent society we tend to look down on littleness: little gifts, little courtesies, little dreams. Maybe these are all that the weary and unbelieving need to draw them back to God again, for in their small way, these little gifts are minute evidences of God's spirit that can grow to illimitable proportions.

We wonder if God has time to answer small prayers, like those of a child, but a child's least prayer is important to God. So are the prayers of all of us. Enough humble prayers, like enough small coins, create a rhythmic flow of a knowledge that God is good and that he hears us.

Under the propulsion of a small event, the world can be changed. The Wright Brothers dreamt of an airplane that would be kept aloft by the upward thrust exerted by the passing of air on its fixed wings and driven by propellers. Their first plane in 1903 was so amateurish that today it looks like a child's plaything, but it has changed the world's transportation system.

Pascal, the great French philosopher and mathematician,

wrote this memorable prayer, "Teach us, O Lord, to do the little things as though they were great, because of the majesty of Christ, who does them in us and who lives our life, and to do the greatest things as though they were little and easy because of his omnipotence."

Chapter 34

Steadfastness in a Widow:
In Christ's Parable

(Luke 18:1–8)

Jesus' parable on the earnestly solicitous widow and the indifferent judge teaches that even though our urgent needs are not met at once we must always pray and not lose heart. This widow came before the judge not once but many times with the same plea: "Vindicate me against my adversary" (Luke 18:3). If widows are poor and burdened like this one, they often lack friends to guide them or the money to pay a judge; so they give up. Yet their needs for counsel can be as imperative as the hunger needs of the poor.

It is easy for an overworked and underpaid judge to become overloaded with the legal needs of others and to be impatient with persistent strangers. This judge was busy, and he refused to listen to the widow. But afterward he said to himself, "Though I neither fear God nor regard man, yet because this widow bothers me, I will vindicate her, or she will wear me out by her continual coming" (Luke 18:4–5).

In three questions Jesus analyzed the meaning of his parable on the importunate widow. First, "Will not God vindicate his elect, who cry to him day and night?" Second, "Will he delay over them?" Jesus' answer to both these questions was immediate and positive: "I tell you, he will vindicate them speedily."

Jesus' third question is more provocative: "When the Son of man comes, will he find faith on earth?" This did not warrant an affirmative answer, for Jesus leads us to believe he will find little faith where he expects it. Few worshipers are as honest and sincere in their faith as they should be.

Jesus used this parable of the importunate widow to make us more aware of our need to pray unceasingly. We must never come before God like beggars or turn aside from God if our prayers are not answered. We must continue to seek him zealously and thank him for what we have.

All our prayers are not answered. Maybe we are unworthy. Maybe we want too much. Maybe we give up when we have to wait too long. If we are as importunate, however, as the widow was, our faith may grow like the grain of mustard seed and bring forth a rich harvest. God promises much. The Book of Psalms is filled with many such promises:

The promise that God blesses the righteous and covers him with favor as with a shield.

The promise that no good thing does the Lord withhold from those who walk uprightly.

The promise that we must wait for the Lord, be strong, and of good courage.

David's plea for vindication is one of the greatest prayers for help in the psalms. He prayed:

> "Prove me, O Lord, and try me;
>   test my heart and my mind.
> For thy steadfast love is before my eyes,
>   and I walk in faithfulness to thee" (Ps. 26:2–3).

Although David had to defend himself and make a final plea for God's help, he prayed on confidently, and finally he had the assurance of an answer. Afterward he gave glory to God and continued to trust him as his rock and fortress.

Even after steadfast prayer, some patriarchs, prophets, and others of faith did not live to see all that was promised. But they are acclaimed in Hebrews 11 as having greeted those promises from afar, knowing that faith "is the assurance of things hoped for, the conviction of things not seen" (Heb. 11:1). They were assured that God had foreseen something better for them.

Section VI

In the Light of Christ and His Church

Light in all its fullness broke forth in the lives of the women around Christ. A radiance surrounded his mother, Mary, and it was especially effulgent among the women who stood beneath him at the cross. A few, like the sinning woman accused of adultery by the scribes and Pharisees, walked away into newness of life after experiencing the presence of Jesus.

In his Mount Olivet discourse, Jesus promised his listeners: "For I will give you . . . wisdom, which none of your adversaries will be able to withstand or contradict" (Luke 21:15).

Paul, Christ's greatest apostle, spoke eloquently of wisdom when he declared: "When I came to you, brethren, I did not come proclaiming to you the testimony of God in lofty words or wisdom. For I decided to know nothing among you except Jesus Christ and him crucified. . . . Yet among the mature we do impart wisdom, although it is not a wisdom of this age or of the rulers of this age, . . . But we impart a secret and hidden wisdom of God, which God decreed before the ages of our glorification" (1 Cor. 2:1–2; 6–7).

Chapter 35

The Mother of a Prophet: *Elizabeth*

(Luke 1:5–80)

"Blessed are you among women, and blessed is the fruit of your womb" (Luke 1:42), exclaimed Elizabeth, when her kinswoman, the mother of Jesus, came to visit her in the hill country of Judah. With Mary's arrival, Elizabeth received special inspiration from the Holy Spirit: "Why is this granted me, that the mother of my Lord should come to me? For behold, when the voice of your greeting came to my ears, the babe in my womb leaped for joy. And blessed is she who believed that there would be a fulfilment of what was spoken to her from the Lord" (Luke 1:43–45).

Elizabeth was six months with child herself. That child would be John the Baptist, a prophet and the forerunner of the Messiah, who would bring the simple message that Jesus is the Christ and that the kingdom of heaven was at hand.

Elizabeth said her son should be called John. Neighbors and relatives wanted to name him Zechariah after his father, a priest, but he also agreed that John should be the child's name. And the New Testament says that "the hand of the Lord was with him" (Luke 1:66), he "grew and became strong in spirit, and he was in the wilderness (Luke 1:80) until he was ready to begin his ministry, and his father Zechariah prophesied, "And you, child, will be called the prophet of the Most High: for you will go before the Lord to prepare his ways" (Luke 1:76).

Jesus honored both Elizabeth and her son when he said, "Among those born of women, there has risen no one greater than John the Baptist" (Matt. 11:11).

In her background and her life Elizabeth was prepared to be the mother of a prophet. She came from the priestly line of Aaron and was the wife of a priest. Like her cousin Mary, she believed that "with God nothing is impossible." It was natural that Elizabeth be the first to hear Mary's Magnificat from her own lips and that Mary stayed with her for three months after her child was conceived.

Elizabeth lived outside the framework of her time and apart from what she saw with her own eyes. Though she dwelt in a material world, her life revolved around spiritual things. And so she spoke to Mary, not as in a dream, but as one certain of what was to come. Who but Elizabeth could have filled Mary's particular need at this time? Elizabeth had to be the one, for she was sure of the power of the Holy Spirit, sure that miracles were possible. What's more, she inspired the three persons closest to her—her husband, her son John, and Mary.

By nature Elizabeth was an inspirer, a humble woman who rose and walked forward fearlessly. She was familiar with the age-old promises of God, and she passed these on to her son.

The pages of history are illuminated by other such mothers: Helena, mother of Constantine the Great, venerated as a saint; Anthusa, the mother of St. John Chrysostom who was a renowned fourth-century preacher and expositor of the Bible; Monica, mother of St. Augustine, whose abiding importance rests on his penetrating understanding of Christian truth; Susanna Wesley, mother of John and Charles her eighteenth child, became England's most gifted hymn writer. John, Susanna's fifteenth child, founded the Methodist movement. These mothers of great sons, like Elizabeth, have kept candles agleam through centuries of Christianity. Helena built the Church of the Nativity at Bethlehem and the Church of the Holy Sepulcher at Jerusalem. Her greatness in later years probably grew out of the suffering she endured when divorced by her son's father. When his father died, her son called her out of obscurity and "ordered that all honor be paid to her as the mother of the sovereign."

Nonna, the mother of Gregory the Divine, acknowledged but one kind of beauty, that of the soul. The only form of noble birth she recognized was goodness.

Monica, the mother of St. Augustine, prayed eighteen years over her son's evil ways. But she saved him for Christianity, and he became one of the greatest men in the church. He is credited with molding the whole of Christian theology from his time in the fourth century down to the thirteenth century.

Anthusa had one objective in educating her son John Chrysostom: to nurture in him the highest qualities of character. She sent him to the celebrated orator Libbanius, and she guided him in his study of the Bible. Furthermore, all her love, care, and wealth were centered on him.

Susanna Wesley's wisdom, stamina, and spiritual sensitivity guided her children to such greatness that her motherhood inspires others whenever her name is mentioned.

Horatius Bonar (1808-1889), Scottish clergyman and hymn writer, brings a special kind of light across the lives of Elizabeth and these other inspirers.

THE MASTER'S TOUCH
In the still air the music lies unheard;
    In the rough marble beauty hides unseen:
To make the music and the beauty, needs,
    The master's touch, the sculptor's chisel
        keen.

Great Master, touch us with Thy skillful hand;
    Let not the music that is in us die!
Great sculptor, hew and polish us; nor let
    Hidden and lost, Thy form within us lie!

Spare not the stroke! do with us as Thou
    wilt!
Let there be naught unfinished, broken,
    marred;
Complete Thy purpose, that we may become
    Thy perfect image, Thou our God and
        Lord!

Chapter 36

The Great Mother:
Mary, the Mother of Jesus

(Luke 1–2)

In mythological, oriental, Jewish, and Christian literature, an aura surrounds the mothers of special children. Mary, the mother of Jesus Christ, is foremost among these.

Born in the image of the invisible God, Jesus Christ arrived on the world scene as a mystery, a new power, a new creation, a gift from the Holy Spirit. Mary, who gave birth to this divine son in such a wondrous manner, has been surrounded from the beginning by a halo of light. As a part of creative nature of the highest order, Mary has been referred to as the citadel for a newly developing body as well as a sanctuary that finally gave that body the power to thrust itself into the world. Now, about two thousand years later, the Christian world is convinced that Mary held within her body a timeless form of life. Only a maiden with the fidelity and faith of Mary could have borne a child of such promise.

Throughout her pregnancy, Mary had the full support of her husband, Joseph. Although most of the time he seemed but a mere bystander, he had the tenderness and beauty of character to give her the protection she needed.

Glorious songs surround Mary's experience. First came the Annunciation of the angel Gabriel. He announced to Mary that she would give birth to the son of the Most High, of whose kingdom there would be no end.

When Mary went to see her cousin Elizabeth, she sang her own Magnificat. Then followed the song of Zechariah, the

Benedictus, in which this father made it known that his son, John the Baptist, would prepare the way for the Lord Jesus. When Mary and Joseph took their child into the Temple at Jerusalem for the first time, Simeon sang what is called the Nunc Dimittis. The angels and shepherds acclaimed Christ's birth by singing, "Glory To God!"

The most remarkable of all these songs is the Magnificat, which has come down to us as the most inspiring message from the heart of a woman that was ever written.

"My soul magnifies the Lord,
and my spirit rejoices in God my Savior,
for he has regarded the low estate of his handmaiden.
For behold, henceforth all generations will call me blessed;
for he who is mighty has done great things for me,
and holy is his name.
And his mercy is on those who fear him
from generation to generation.
He has shown strength with his arm,
for he has scattered the proud in the imagination of their hearts,
he has put down the mighty from their thrones,
and exalted those of low degree;
he has filled the hungry with good things,
and the rich he has sent empty away.
He has helped his servant Israel,
in remembrance of his mercy,
as he spoke to our fathers,
to Abraham and to his posterity for ever" (Luke 1:46–55).

The Magnificat is in reality a psalm, modeled after the Old Testament psalms. Hannah's song before the birth of Samuel is also a psalm.

Mary's Song is best understood when divided into strophes of two or more verses each; each division is a complete idea unto itself. In the first, Mary praises God. In the second, she dwells on her part as the mother of the incarnate Son. In the third, she rises to the larger view of God's place in history. In the fourth, she comes back to the thought of the messianic time and the assurance that God's promise will be fulfilled.

The song of Mary is more than a psalm and something less than a complete Christian hymn. Mary had within her a consciousness of the nearness to the fulfillment of this promise; yet she did not speak of the promised one by his human name or refer to the mysteries of his life, death, and resurrection. Her song, rather, presents a particular moment of transition in sacred history when the twilight of the past is disappearing into the dawn of the new day.

Mary was reborn when she received the Annunciation. Her dialogue in the Magnificat reached a new plateau as if God had put into her mouth the exact words. Whether Mary wrote this song or not, no one knows, but she was the key figure in its emergence from thoughts into words.

Faith has been well defined as the believer's act of enlightened belief in God and God's ability to fulfill his promises. In Mary's act of faith after the Annunciation, she emerged into a new being. During her pregnancy and the birth of her son, she was sure that God had taken the initiative in her life. She asked no questions but rushed to give God the full credit, for she had felt his presence from the moment of her son's conception until the time of his birth. Not only was she assured that God could exalt the humble, but she knew that his mercy would be upon all who feared him.

It is often easier to believe the unseen possibility of God's power to transform the life in a humble young woman like Mary than it is to understand profound theological discussions. Mary's simple faith lifted her into a great miracle, unexplainable but real nevertheless. Mary showed a quick understanding of the things of God, but she was also aware that her own knowledge was finite at best. She perceived that through Christ many would come to understand better the infinite essence of God and what he meant us to be.

Mary's feminine-maternal wisdom was not a disinterested knowledge but a loving participation, for she nourished in her body a life of the spirit.

There is a mystical grandeur about Mary, who carried the wondrous light of God within her being. She was miraculously lifted to a higher plane, where her maternity and spirituality came together into an indefinable whole. If there ever was a time when the mothers of children yet to be born need to absorb Mary's lowly, believing attitude and her explicit faith in God's promises, it is now. She seems to tell us that only a handful of believing mothers and fathers can change the world for the better.

Chapter 37

The Foresight of a Saint:
Anna, the Prophetess

(Luke 2:36–38)

The aged Anna was one of the saints in the Jerusalem Temple. She was familiar no doubt with the prophecy of Isaiah 53. She knew that the Redeemer of Israel would come and that his life would be regarded as a tragic failure but that his death, as seen by God, would be a glorious success.

From the moment the child Jesus was brought into the Temple by his parents, Anna recognized him as the Redeemer of whom Isaiah had spoken. It is no wonder that Mary understood what Simeon meant when he later prophesied, "A sword will pierce through your own soul also."

The devout Anna was prepared for her exalting role, for she fasted night and day and gave thanks to God for sending this child. Anna, who lived for others, typified the Jerusalem Temple woman at her noblest. She was one of those rare beings who finds her main reason for existence in praising God.

> "One thing have I asked of the Lord,
>   that I will seek after,
> that I may dwell in the house of the Lord
>   all the days of my life,
> to behold the beauty of the Lord,
>   and to inquire in his temple" (Ps. 27:4).

Anna probably lived in the Temple after she became a widow. If she did not live there, she spent more time there than anywhere else. She hid there in times of trouble, sang to God there

in times of joy. It is not surprising that Anna should be the first
to declare Christ as the long awaited Redeemer of her people.
She had opened a door for Christ's New Testament church to
come.

Anna makes us certain that devout women have a heritage in
religion "to regain, develop and carry forward," as stated so well
by Margaret Brackenbury Crook in her book *Women and
Religion* (Beacon Press, 1964, pp. 249-51). Mrs. Crook, who
has taught Old Testament studies in universities in this country
and abroad, is well prepared to speak on women's innate, life-
conserving capacities and intuitive insights to meet the needs in
religion today. She tells us,

> The Universe has outrun our computations. We are being invited
> to move to new experiences, and new attempts at definition of God's
> part and our own. We stand at the opening of a new era in religion. . . .
> We have to win our emancipation from bondage to ancient concepts
> without losing our sense of being at home in the universe. . . . This,
> too, is part of our heritage. Although our predecessors were naive
> about it, they were wholeheartedly at home in the universe as they
> knew it.

"God has not changed, since the early Temple experience of
Anna, but we have changed. And we must be willing to share in
molding the spiritual life of our time, for women and men bear
the same responsibility. Our service may seem infinitesimal, like
the ripple of a tiny rock thrown into a deep sea, but that ripple
can reach a wave and wash into a breaker."

In most of our seemingly insignificant contributions to that
which is good, we come to understand better these two hymnal
verses by Walter Chamber Smith (1824-1908) sung to an old
Welsh melody.

> Immortal, invisible, God only wise,
> In light inaccessible hid from our eyes,
> Most blessed, most glorious, the Ancient of Days,
> Almighty, victorious, Thy great Name we praise.
>
> Unresting, unhasting, and silent as light
> Nor wanting nor wasting, Thou rulest in might;
> Thy justice like mountains high soaring above
> Thy clouds which are fountains of goodness and love.
> To all, life Thou givest—to both great and small;
> In all light Thou livest, the true life of all.

Chapter 38

Power Through Believing:
Women at Sick Bed and Grave

Jesus' words to the sick and dying are affirmations of faith. Sometimes he merely came into their presence, and sometimes he only saw them from afar. Whatever the procedure, the healed and the onlookers were filled with a sense of wonder.

Simon Peter's mother-in-law had a high fever, and Jesus only stood by and gently touched her hand. The fever left, and she rose and served him.

To the woman who had hemorrhaged for twelve years, Jesus declared, "Take heart, daughter; your faith has made you well" (Matt. 9:22). The woman had only felt his touch, but she perceived his power and was restored.

For the epileptic son, Jesus had a word of encouragement. When the disciples asked why they could not cast out the demon causing the disease, Jesus answered, "Because of your little faith. For truly, I say to you, if you have faith as a grain of mustard seed, you will say to this mountain, 'Move hence to yonder place,' and it will move; and nothing will be impossible to you" (Matt. 17:20–21).

To the woman crooked in body for eighteen years, Jesus spoke, "Woman, you are freed from your infirmity.' And he laid his hand upon hjer, and immediately she was made straight" (Luke 13:12-13).

Christ's raising of the dead was even more miraculous. When he arrived at the home of the ruler whose daughter lay dead, he silenced the flute players and the crowd making a tumult over her death. Then he spoke firmly, "Depart, for the girl is not dead but sleeping." Then he took her hand, and she arose.

To the widow of Nain, whose only son had died and was being carried out to be buried, Jesus said, "Do not weep." And he came and touched the bier and said, "Young man, I say to you arise!" The young man sat up and began to speak.

Lazarus, the brother of Martha and Mary, had been in the tomb four days. Jesus first said to Martha, "'Your brother will rise again. . . . I am the resurrection and the life; he who believes in me, though he die, yet shall he live, and whoever lives and believes in me shall never die. Do you believe this?' She said to him, 'Yes, Lord; I believe that you are the Christ, the Son of God, he who is coming into the world'" (John, 11:22–27).

When Jesus walked with Martha to meet Mary at the tomb, Mary repeated the same words as Martha, "Lord, if you had been here, my brother would not have died" (Luke 11:32).

For once Jesus himself wept at what he saw: the grieved sisters, whom he loved, and their weeping friends. When he came to the grave itself, he asked that the stone be removed. Then he lifted up his eyes and said, "Father, I thank thee that thou hast heard me. I knew that thou hearest me always, but I have said this on account of the people standing by, that they may believe that thou didst send me." After this he said in a loud voice, "Lazarus, come out," and he did, his hands and feet bound with bandages, and his face wrapped with a cloth. Jesus said to those near the grave, "Unbind him, and let him go" (John 11:41–44).

Without science and scholarship, Jesus shed more light on things human and divine than all the philosophers and scholars combined. To the sick and the dying he imparted what Paul called "a secret and hidden wisdom of God, which God decreed before the ages for our glorification" (1 Cor. 2:7).

His healings and his raising of the dead were among his greatest miracles; yet his moral and spiritual revelations of God took precedence over these. The revelations were the gateway he opened to a new and higher order, leading us on to a knowledge of the inner man, a fuller understanding of the soul, man's inmost self, the seat of his immortality.

Whatever Jesus did, he expressed his utmost dependence upon God, the father of all knowledge and the source of his strength. Jesus also had great rapport with suffering humanity.

His healings expressed that rapport, a form of spiritual energy in itself.

It was Jesus' conviction that disease and suffering are not a part of the natural order of life. He knew too the power of the mind over the body, and he labored to produce faith in that power. He freed the sick of their hopelessness and depression and dealt with their hidden sins, as if these could be at the root of some of their trouble.

In time of sickness and death, when we draw nearer him, we understand the source of his power. We know that no one can do these miracles "unless God is with him." So miracles are not only signs of wonder but also outward expressions of one's desire to live nearer God.

Charles Kingsley, the English clergyman, 1819-1875, wrote these inspiring thoughts:

THE GREAT PHYSICIAN
From Thee all skill and science flow,
   All pity, care and love.
All calm and courage, faith and hope;
   O pour them from above.

And part them, Lord, to each and all,
   As each and all shall need,
To rise like incense, each to Thee,
   In noble thought and deed.

And hasten, Lord, that perfect day
   When pain and death shall cease,
And Thy just rule shall fill the earth
   With health and light and peace.

Chapter 39

On Mercy:
The Mother of an Afflicted Child

(Matt. 15:21–28; Mark 7:24–30)

"Have mercy on us, O Lord; my daughter is severely afflicted with a demon," begged the wise Canaanite woman when she came before Jesus on his visit to Tyre and Sidon. She probably was a poor beggar woman, whom no one except Jesus would notice. Even his disciples were irritated that she should plead so loudly for help.

"Send her away, for she is crying after us," the disciples said to Jesus.

But she came back a second time, "Lord help me."

After testing her, Jesus found she had wit, spirit, and faith. "O woman, great is your faith. Be it done for you as you desire," he told her.

She turned toward home, joyous in spirit and richer in faith; and when she arrived, she found her child lying in bed. The demon had vanished, as if it had never been present.

The dialogue between this mother and Jesus still rings in the hearts of parents everywhere who suffer over birth defects in their children, such as mental retardation, cerebral palsy, or learning or walking disabilities, all an unending strain on mother and child.

Demons, as they were called in Bible times, truly were evil spirits. They were difficult to conquer because they were mixed up with emotional and physical disturbances. Parents today suffer in the same way as this Canaanite woman. The main difference between the parents of an afflicted child now and then is that today they usually turn first to a social service agency and finally, after long waiting, to a home for afflicted children.

But with such demands for help increasing in an ever-growing urban population, parents may cry for help and never receive any. Often they suffer alone and without experiencing compassion from either outsiders or her family.

Such mothers can become so distraught and feel so hopeless that, in desperation and distress they turn to liquor or drugs for relief. If they are not careful their condition can become as bad or worse than the child's.

While living daily with an afflicted child, it is almost impossible to prove one's faith without outside spiritual help. This usually comes first from a minister, but he or she is usually loaded down with the cares of many families. A psychiatrist may help also, but he or she has human limitations.

Each of us should ask ourselves how merciful we are to those with heartbreaking afflictions. If we communicate to them a spirit of love and mercy, we can help a little.

"Surely goodness and mercy shall follow me all the days of my life" (Ps. 23:6). This verse does not apply only to our needs, but we can extend its power to others who need us. The mercy of God does not work in a vacuum but in the example of Christ through those who possess his spirit. Early in his ministry Christ made it known that he desired mercy, not sacrifice.

In his efforts among the poor, the needy, and the afflicted, Jesus proved that God's mercy seeks a higher good than the temporary relief of distress. Mercy signifies love to one another, the kind of love Jesus showed the grieving mother.

How great it is to live in that steadfast love of God. One can take refuge in God's mercy, for it is one of his essential qualities, and it never ends. If you and I are to act as children of God, we must be merciful to all alike, even the sinning and the ungrateful, doing unto them as we would have them do unto us. Wherever we stand we must learn through our own suffering that mercy is truly the essence of the teaching of God and his son, Jesus Christ. "Blessed are the merciful, for they shall obtain mercy" (Matt. 5:7). "But I have trusted in thy mercy; my heart shall rejoice in thy salvation. I will sing unto the Lord, because he hath dealt bountifully with me. (Ps. 13:5-6, KJV).

Spiritual Preparation:
The Wise Virgins

(Matt. 25:1–13)

"The kingdom of heaven shall be compared to ten maidens who took their lamps and went to meet the bridegroom. Five of them were foolish, and five were wise. For when the foolish took their lamps, they took no oil with them; but the wise took flasks of oil with their lamps" (Matt. 25:1-4).

In this parable of the wise and foolish virgins, Jesus taught the contrast between diligent preparation and carelessness. He wanted all believers to know that they should watch and be prepared for the coming of the Lord.

In this case the five wise young maidens were ready to go forward with the bridegroom to the marriage feast. Although he was late, they had trimmed their lamps and filled them with oil to await his coming. But the foolish virgins, awakening suddenly from their slumber, said to the wise ones, "Give us some of your oil, for our lamps are going out." But the wise replied, "Perhaps there will not be enough for us and for you."

Because they were prepared, the wise maidens went in with the bridegroom, Christ himself, to the marriage feast. When they were there, the door was shut. The foolish maidens arrived late and asked, "Lord, lord open to us," but the bridegroom replied, "I do not know you. Watch therefore for later, for you know neither the day nor the hour when I will call again."

Preparation is a theme that runs through the Bible. In the Old Testament it often refers to preparation for war, however the psalms sing of preparing for the way of the Lord. Amos was the first to declare, "Prepare to meet your Lord." Finally Malachi, the last of the prophets, told us, "Behold, I will send my messenger, and he shall prepare the way before me."

Spiritual preparation reaches its highest peak in the New Testament. Here we become more conscious of the preparation of the spiritually faithful and the unpreparedness of the faithless. The latter have not broken up the fallow ground or purged out the old leaven or trimmed their lamps and filled them with oil.

But great promises are there for those who have. The eye has not seen nor the ear heard, neither has there entered into our hearts the things that God has prepared for those who love him. The promise is that "God has revealed to us through the Spirit" (1 Cor. 2:10). The one who is prepared is like a vessel sanctified, ready for the master's use and ready for every good work (see 2 Tim. 2:21).

We sometimes get our priorities mixed up. We are so absorbed in obtaining our rights, in caring for our families, in earning a living, that we easily fall asleep spiritually. Then when the storms of life come, we suddenly see that we have slighted spiritual preparedness. Even the tiny ant, according to Proverbs, prepared her food in the summer and gathered her sustenance in harvest. In his warning against idleness, the writer of Proverbs reminds us:

> "Go to the ant, O sluggard;
> consider her ways, and be wise. . . .
> How long will you lie there, O sluggard?
> When will you arise from your sleep?" (Prov. 6:6-9).

In his parable of the wise and foolish virgins, Jesus, of course, is referring to spiritual preparedness, which is far more important than material preparedness. However, even in the time of Jesus, few understood this. One of these was the proud and ambitious mother Salome, who begged for recognition for her sons James and John, two of the twelve disciples. With them she went before Jesus, knelt down, and asked, " 'Command that these two sons of mine may sit, one at your right hand and one at your left, in your kingdom.' But Jesus answered, 'You do not know what you are asking. Are you able to drink the cup that I am to drink?' They said to him, 'We are able.' He said to them, 'You will drink my cup, but . . . it is for those for whom it has been prepared by my Father' " (Matt. 20:21-23).

Most of us are like this mother and her two sons. We assume we are ready, but we have no idea of what spiritual preparedness means. We forget that spiritual greatness is not given but earned through sacrifice and suffering.

Chapter 41

In the World of the Spirit:
Jesus and the Woman at the Well

(John 4:7–42)

When the Samaritan woman came to draw water at Jacob's well at Sychar, she found Jesus sitting there, weary from a journey he was making to Galilee. His disciples had gone into the city to buy food, and he was famished for water; so he asked her for a drink. But the woman questioned him about why he should ask her for a drink of water when he was a Jew and she was a Samaritan, a people disliked by the Jews.

Jesus answered her, "If you knew the gift of God, and who it is that is saying to you, 'Give me a drink,' you would have asked him, and he would have given you living water" (John 4:10).

Said the woman to him, "Sir, you have nothing to draw with, and the well is deep; where do you get that living water?" (4:11).

Jesus answered, "Every one who drinks of this water will thirst again, but whoever drinks of the water that I shall give him will never thirst; the water that I shall give him will become in him a spring of water welling up to eternal life" (4:13).

The woman then begged Jesus to give her some of that living water so that she would not thirst again or come here to draw water.

He said to her, "Go, call your husband, and come here." The woman then told him she had no husband. Spoke Jesus, "You are right, you have had five husbands, and this one you now have is not your husband." The woman then perceived that Jesus was a prophet. The climax came when Jesus, in his discourse with the woman said, "The hour is coming, and now is, when the true worshipers will worship the Father in spirit and truth, for such the Father seeks to worship him. God is a spirit, and those who worship him must worship in spirit and truth" (4:23-24).

The woman continued in the discourse with Jesus, "I know that Messiah is coming (he who is called Christ); when he comes, he will show us all things" (4:25). Jesus startled her when he said, "I who speak to you am he" (4:26).

Her thoughts suddenly began to soar so high that she longed to share with others what she had learned from Christ. She went forth hastily to become a sower and reaper, ready to gather souls into what have been called "the granaries of heaven," where living water and the bread of life are available in abundance.

This woman of Samaria left her water pot and went to tell the village people about the Messiah and what he had told her. Soon they came streaming from the village to see the man who proclaimed he was the Messiah. In turn he visited with them for two days.

Then they said to the woman, "It is no longer because of your words that we believe, for we have heard for ourselves, and we know that this is indeed the Savior of the world" (4:42).

The spiritual lesson of living water takes us into another dimension of the Spirit. Water was valued in these times because it was scarce. It is mentioned more often in the Bible than any other natural resource. The Israelites, wandering in the desert, came upon twelve springs of water. At God's direction, Moses struck a rock, and water flowed from it. In the New Testament, water became a symbol of baptism. "Unless one is born of water [baptism] and the Spirit, he cannot enter the kingdom of God" (John 3:5), Jesus told Nicodemus. Water became a symbol of the eternal life that wells up within the converted. The woman at the well experienced this symbolism in all its fullness when Christ conversed with her.

In the space age, illuminated by new discoveries, in galaxies in the far reaches of space, wonders that awe the imagination await us! The woman at the well was limited in her concept of space, confined as it was in Bible times to the firmament, the vault of heaven, where the sun, the moon, and the stars were mere shining specks in the distance. But now man has walked on the moon, and it is no longer a speck but the earth's natural satellite.

Suddenly the great spaces beyond the firmament seem linked with our own destiny and with God. The Holy Spirit that Jesus told the woman at the well about seems even more omnipotent and omniscient than it was conceived in Bible times. But we are prone, just as the woman of Samaria, to become so involved in our own problems and trivia that we permit them to hedge us in from the wonders about us and from the even greater wonders far out in space beyond our vision. Only for a few years have we looked far into the many galaxies beyond, but these years are only moments in the aeons of time.

This woman who had lived with six different men, none of whom was her husband, was so encumbered by materiality that she was blinded to the world of the spirit. But Jesus awakened in her a relationship to God, the eternal spirit.

Amid the scientific discoveries in the age of space, we can better sense the meaning of Christ's discourse to this woman at the well because we catch a glimpse of God's ever-expanding handiwork.

At least the search has begun out in space, and the many galaxies, isolated from similar systems by vast regions of space, seem to be speeding us into a greater knowledge of the infinite reaches of the universe. From our own frontier on planet Earth, we come to understand better the first verse of Genesis: "In the beginning God created the heavens and the earth. The earth was without form and void, and darkness was upon the face of the deep; and the Spirit of God was moving over the face of the waters." Astronomers now describe the regions of space between countless galaxies as being "without form and void."

Are other intelligent beings out there among the stars? Does only this void of interstellar density separate us from them? Are there extraterrestial civilizations out there searching for us too?

These questions remain unanswered. We only know that Christ unfolded before the eyes of the woman at the well this marvelous concept of God as a spirit. Christ saw her rush forth as a new child of God prepared for a new life in a new dimension of thought. Now she wanted to rush back and share her new knowledge with others.

Like this woman, we may not understand all the new wonders in this ever-changing universe, but we feel ourselves being touched by new wings that cause our spirits to soar. Through the experience of the woman of Samaria, we also come closer to Christ who "reflects the glory of God and bears the very stamp of his nature, upholding the universe by his word of power" (Heb. 1:3). Because we understand better, we rejoice more too in this revelation:

> "'What no eye has seen, nor ear heard,
>   nor the heart of man conceived,
>   what God has prepared for those who love him,'
>   God has revealed to us through the Spirit. For the
> Spirit searches everything, even the depths of God" (1 Cor. 2:9–10).

The woman of Samaria received from Christ a unique gift never bestowed upon woman before. When He imparted something of God's Spirit to her, she went forth a new person.

Chapter 42

The Accused and Accusers
The Sinning Woman

(John 8:3–11)

"Woman, where are your accusers? Has no man condemned you? She answered, "No man, Lord, and Jesus said unto her, neither do I condemn you; go and sin no more" (John 8:10-11).

The scribes and Pharisees brought to Jesus a woman caught in the act of adultery, as if they were helping him. Smugly, they reminded Jesus that, according to the old Law of Moses, the woman should be stoned to death; and they, thinking themselves better than she, were ready to stone her.

The compassionate Jesus was silent toward them at first. Then he stooped down and wrote on the ground, as if he had not heard them. Finally he told them, "He that is without sin among you, let him first cast a stone at her" (John 8:7, KJV).

Convicted of their sin by their own guilty consciences, they disappeared one by one as Jesus and the woman talked together. The scribes and Pharisees had judged the woman according to the world. But Jesus, knowing that he would die for the sins of others like these, made it known for the first time that where he would go, they could not come.

Jesus possessed human and divine wisdom. His human wisdom is expressed in his knowledge of the Scriptures and his power to interpret them, in his deep moral insight gained by the actual experiences of temptation and suffering, in his capacity for learning in the synagogue when he was a boy, in his common sense, practical ability, and the skill to construct a parable, and in his capacity for asking the right questions.

In the case of the woman caught in adultery, he showed human wisdom by first remaining silent before the accusers, who could not refute what he finally said. Christ's divine wisdom came through the spirit of God, speaking to and through him. And he promised: "I will give you a mouth and wisdom, which none of your adversaries will contradict . . . By your endurance you will gain your lives" (Luke 20:15, 19).

Throughout history women, too often referred to as the weaker sex, have suffered unjust accusals. As in this instance the man caught in the act of adultery with her is not even mentioned; yet he was guilty too, and the old Levitical law clearly states that both the man and woman shall be punished when caught in adultery. Bereaved and deprived women often suffer legal injustice, for it is easier to denounce than to show compassion, more popular to throw stones than to give a fair trial.

Jesus scoffed at a holier-than-thou attitude, of which we all are guilty. Too often we practice a religion not of the heart but of ceremony, not of reason but of form, not of God but of creed.

This sinning woman may have had more real love and compassion for others than her accusers. Jesus knew this. If we are to grow spiritually, we have to learn to be whole, not Christians in name only. Regardless of our status and our church affiliation, we must never forget we can all be one in Christ. In that is hope for the accuser and the accused.

"He who belittles his neighbor lacks sense,
    but a man of understanding remains silent.
He who goes about as a talebearer reveals secrets,
    but he who is trustworthy in spirit keeps a thing hidden" (Prov. 11:12-13).

Chapter 43

Love in Action:
Mary of Bethany

(Matt. 26:6–13; Mark 14:3–9; John 12:1–8)

"'Why this waste? For this ointment might have been sold for a large sum, and given to the poor!' But Jesus, aware of this, said to them, 'Why do you trouble the woman? For she has done a beautiful thing to me. For you always have the poor with you, but you will not always have me. . . . Truly, I say to you, wherever this gospel is preached in the whole world, what she has done will be told in memory of her" (Matt. 26:8-13).

Mary of Bethany had a close fellowship with Jesus. He had revealed himself to her in his toils, conflicts, and suffering. Who he was and where his power came from was a mystery to many, but not to Mary of Bethany. When he raised her brother Lazarus from the tomb, she had the spiritual discernment to understand his love in action to others. And she gave Jesus back the same kind of love in this, her last opportunity to serve him.

What she did for Christ six days before the Passover, when she anointed him, went beyond that moment of time into eternity. It exemplified the meaning of true giving and enabled others to see that unselfish love is eternal. She was willing to prove her love, no matter what the material cost of the jar of pure nard (about sixty dollars then, but far more now).

On the other hand, Judas Iscariot, one of the twelve apostles, went before the chief priests to betray Jesus. He received from them thirty pieces of silver, or about one-third of what Mary's gift was worth. These coins became a curse to Judas, who died a self-inflicted death; the money Mary had spent on the costly ointment became a blessing to her memory.

Judas' act represented hate and a misplaced power in action. It brought good to no one, only death to himself, because he could not live with himself. Mary's gift represented love at its best. She knew that Christians must suffer much but that the pangs of that suffering were lessened if Christians remained kind and loving toward one another.

Mary was assured in her heart that Jesus would valiantly go forward to suffer because he who was born in the image of God believed all things—even that death could be overcome—hoped for all things—even eternal life—and was willing to endure all things—even death on the cross.

Love to Mary of Bethany was not just a part of her existence; it was the very breath of her life.

Lydia H. Sigourney, an American writer of more than a century ago, said that "the soul of woman lives in love." Mary's act exemplified this, for she reflected God's image in her very being, a quality Martin Luther called "the living essence of the divine nature which beams full of all goodness."

Chapter 44

Christian Devotion:
Many Women Were There

(Matt. 27:55–56; Luke 23:55, 24:1–30

"There were also many women there, looking on from afar, who had followed Jesus from Galilee, ministering to him" (Matt. 27:55).

The many women at Jesus' crucifixion and burial set an example for caring women everywhere—women who go forward without being asked and prepare food for the sick, call at the home of a family who has lost a loved one, stand at the graveside to comfort the sorrowing.

These words from the nineteenth-century clergyman and author Edward Everett Hale speak to the helper as well as to the one helped.

> LEND A HAND
> I am only one,
> But still I am one;
> I cannot do everything,
> But still I can do something;
> And because I cannot do everything
> I will not refuse to do the something
>   that I can do.

Simon of Cyrene, who picked up Jesus' cross and carried it all the way to Golgotha, was so helpful that he is memorialized as one who voluntarily performed a seemingly small but meaningful service to Jesus without complaining and without fanfare. In a world of sprawling cities, where people get lost, crosses too heavy to bear often disappear from view.

The women who walked all the way with Jesus knew that he needed their spiritual inspiration as well as Simon's physical support. Christ in his agony could not speak to any of them, but when he glanced up at them, he knew they cared deeply. Like Simon, these women did not ask what they could do, but when the need arose, they voluntarily went forward and walked all the way to the cross.

These dedicated women tell us how to serve the sorrowing. They make us know that one's presence in a room of grieving loved ones can be a balm of peace. Some of us put too little emphasis on thoughtfulness to the grief-stricken. Perhaps we do not know how best to show love to others, or perhaps we get our priorities mixed up and turn to trivial pursuits.

Not until sorrow comes our way do we learn what caring friends and family can mean. Through them and with them we experience a real fellowship of love. In timid moments, when we falter in showing care, we need to draw closer to the devoted women who not only walked near Christ as he went to his death but who agonized over his suffering at the cross and who grieved for him at the tomb until they learned he had risen. They were blessed tenfold because they were among the first to understand the power of the cross and the wonder of the resurrection.

Chapter 45

On Forgiving:
The Woman with Alabaster

(Luke 7:36–50)

The story of the gift of this woman, identified only as the sinning woman, bears a striking resemblance to the gift of Mary of Bethany, but neither woman bore the slightest likeness to the other. Only their gifts were similar. Each brought ointment to Jesus and anointed him before the crucifixion. The sinning woman, it is clearly stated, brought her ointment in a flask of alabaster.

Mary of Bethany brought her ointment to Jesus while he was at the home of Simon the leper, whom he had healed. This other woman brought her ointment to the home of Simon, the Pharisees, a society of zealous students and teachers of the Law, whose emphasis on harsh and uncharitable legalities always came ahead of emphasis on the loving nature of God the Father.

The theme of both of these anointment stories centers around love and forgiveness. The sinning woman, weeping because of her sins, stood behind Jesus at a table. She paused to wet his feet with her tears, to wipe them with the hair of her head, and to kiss them and anoint them.

Those sitting by, including Simon the Pharisee, were alarmed that Jesus would permit a sinning woman to touch him. But he forgave her sins and accepted her gift as an act of her inner faith.

"Your sins are forgiven. . . . Your faith has saved you; go in peace" (Luke 7:48, 50), he told her.

Jesus preceded his remarks to this woman with a parable spoken especially for Simon.

"'A certain creditor had two debtors; one owed five hundred denarii, and the other fifty. When they could not pay, he forgave them both. Now which of them will love him more?' Simon answered, 'The one, I suppose, to whom he forgave more'" (Luke 7:41-43).

Jesus told Simon that he had judged rightly and then went on to explain that this woman's sins, "which are many, are forgiven, for she loved much; but he who is forgiven little, loves little" (Luke 7:47).

Giving brings out a variety of responses in both the giver and the receiver. The gift of Mary of Bethany to Jesus is a lasting memorial to her. The gift of the sinning woman to him is a lasting tribute to faith. Each gift had deep meaning, for gratitude sings praises to God. Gratitude itself is an obligation, incumbent upon all of us, but in larger measure upon one who receives a pardon along with appreciation for a gift.

The similar gifts of both the Sinning Woman and Mary of Bethany suggest the following of Kahlil Gibran's, *The Prophet* (New York, 1971, p. 20). He says in part,

ON GIVING

There are those who give little of the much which they have—and they give it for recognition and their hidden desire makes their gifts unwholesome.

And there are those who have little and give it all.

These are the believers in life and the bounty of life, and their coffer is never empty.

There are those who give with joy, and that joy is their reward.

And there are those who give with pain, and that pain is their baptism.

And there are those who give and know not pain in giving, nor do they seek joy, nor give with mindfulness of virtue;

They give as in yonder valley the myrtle breathes its fragrance into space.

Through the hands of such as these God speaks, and from behind their eyes He smiles upon the earth.

Chapter 46

A Woman's Intuition: *Pilate's Wife*

(Matt. 27:19–26)

When Pilate, the Roman governor of Judaea, was presiding over the chief priests and elders of the people who had taken counsel against Jesus to put him to death, he received this urgent message from his wife: "Have nothing to do with that righteous man, for I have suffered much over him today in a dream" (Matt. 27:19).

Already in chains, Jesus was up for the death sentence because he had declared himself the Messiah (king of the Jews). No doubt Pilate was aware that it was out of envy that the mob had delivered Jesus to him, also that not a single charge had been brought against him.

Before the message arrived, there was some question as to whether the Sannhedrin should release Jesus or the notorious prisoner Barabbas, a murderer and a revolutionary. Pilate had already asked, "Whom do you want me to release for you, Barabbas, or Jesus who is called Christ?"

The crowds shouted "Barabbas." And they then thundered, "Crucify Jesus."

A riot was developing, and Pilate's wife sensed the mood of the people gathered about her husband. She must have known that when Jesus arrived in her husband's court he was already bound in the trappings of a common prisoner, that Judas Iscariot the betrayer, had brought back to the court thirty pieces of silver and had openly confessed, "I have sinned in betraying innocent blood."

One can easily surmise that all these events had caused the discerning wife of Pilate to be fearful about her husband's part in accusing a man as just as Jesus. It would be natural for a conscientious wife to have bad dreams while her husband presided over court proceedings of one she knew to be unjustly accused.

The intuitive sense of a perceptive woman like Pilate's wife is often God-given and demands attention, but listeners often scoff at such counsel, wise or not, and do as they please. Eloise Hackett has an interesting commentary on this:

CONVENTIONALITY
Men wrap themselves in smug cocoons
Of dogmas they believe are wise,
and look askance at one who sees
in worms potential butterflies.

Although Pilate's wife saw emerging an opportunity for her husband to save this good man, he chose to wrap himself in a "smug cocoon." The disruptive conditions of his time demanded this choice. As the riot around Jesus grew stronger, Pilate gave up, and soon Jesus was on the way to the cross.

The tragedy that came to Jesus might have been averted had Pilate heeded his wife's advice. Her actions challenge us to seek greater insight into God's will and to speak up when we feel we are right. Others may scoff—they might scoff anyway—but on faith, courage, and confidence we can press forward to aid the oppressed. In this case the Roman leaders were powerful enough to sway history in their direction. The voice of one lone woman was not enough to drown out the voices of the noisy mob.

Pilate's wife failed because she was the victim of political forces stronger than she was, forces that were determined to do away with "that righteous man." This was all in God's plan and one lone woman could not change that. But we have to admire anyone who speaks against evil, who is at least not afraid to try.

Isabella of Castille (1451-1504), queen of Spain, prayed for the grace to rule and to use well the authority God had given her. Intricate problems surrounded her throne, but she had confidence that God would guide her, and he did. One of her prayers lives on as a symbol of her suffering and her conquest:

I beseech Thee, Lord, to hear the prayer of Thy servant. Show forth thy truth and manifest Thy will with Thy marvelous works.

Give me wisdom and courage to move forward with the aid of Thine arm alone.

And yet Isabella was a realist. She did not leave everything to God. "In all human affairs," she said, "there are things both certain and doubtful, and both are equally in the hands of God, who is accustomed to guide to a good end the causes that are just and are sought with diligence."

Chapter 47

On Faithfulness:
Joanna

(Luke 8:3, 24:10)

Joanna was among that small group of women, honored as "one of the saints in Christ Jesus," about whom Paul spoke in the salutation of Ephesians. She was destined in love to be Christ's own and still lives on "for the purpose of his glory."

Joanna was one of the women who went to the tomb to embalm the body of Jesus and found that he had arisen. The apostles had left after the burial, but a handful of women were faithful until the resurrection, three days later. When the apostles heard Mary Magdalene's announcement, they thought it an idle tale fabricated by women, but then they went and saw the empty tomb themselves.

Little is known about the personal life of Joanna, except that she was the wife of Chuza, Herod's steward, and that her name appears among those other women "of means," who were faithful to Christ throughout his ministry.

What is most significant is that Joanna gave spiritual comfort to Christ as well as of her material means. Her faithfulness to him clarifies his parable that comes in the verse in Luke right after her name.

"A sower went out to sow his seed: and as he sowed, some fell along the path, and was trodden under foot, and the birds of the air devoured it. And some fell on the rock; and as it grew up, it withered away, because it had no moisture. And some fell among thorns; and the thorns grew with it and choked it. Some fell into good soil and grew, and yielded a hundredfold" (Luke 8:5-8).

Joanna "fell into good soil," grew spiritually, and yielded a hundredfold. Because she did not hold her light under a bushel, her life has lighted the path of believers for centuries. Her faith came from above, and it had great power, making us sure "the Lord preserves the faithful."

Without our faithful Joannas—humble, serene, believing women—there would be little hope for the downhearted overtaken by insurmountable problems. Without their kind of faithfulness, "reaching to the clouds," as the psalmist described it, the world would be a dreary place. But the faithful ones like Joanna carry a light that dispels the darkness wherever they go.

Often these Joannas are right beside us, but we don't recognize their worth because we are looking for those with big names, palatial houses, spectacular careers. We forget that Joannas walk by faith, not by sight. They know that "faith is the assurance of things hoped for, the conviction of things not seen" (Heb. 11:1).

Chapter 48

At the Threshold:
Mary Magdalene

(John 19:25, 20:11–18)

When Mary Magdalene hurried to the disciples to report the miracle of the resurrection, she carried with her the foundation of the New Testament church. Without her and the women about her, the drama of the death and resurrection of Christ would not have been the same. Nor would the church have had such a solid base or such a congregation of believers as represented by the many women who were at the crucifixion and the resurrection.

Mary Magdalene had been healed by Jesus of a possible emotional disturbance, and she loved him with a holy love. It was natural that she would spread the first message of his resurrection because she was faithful to the end. She was not included among the disciples. No woman was. But that does not matter. She was included in his circle of love, and she led the way for others.

When Christ arose, Mary Magdalene was the first person to whom he spoke, and he called her by name. She turned to him with a cry of recognition, "Rabboni" (meaning "teacher").

Jesus said to her, "Do not hold me, for I have not yet ascended to . . . my Father and your Father, to my God and your God" (John 20:17).

Mary Magdalene rushed to the disciples to say, "'I have seen the Lord'; and she told them that he had said these things to her" (20:18).

Mary Magdalene's ministry to Jesus makes us appreciate all

the more these words by Georgia Harkness, American clergyman, educator, and author, in:

THE UNDERSTANDING HEART
Give me, O God, the understanding heart—
The quick discernment of the soul to see
Another's inner wish the hidden part
Of him, who wordless, speaks for sympathy.
I would be kind, but kindness is not all:
In arid places may I find the wells,
The deeps within my neighbor's soul that call
To me, and lead me where his spirit dwells.
When Jesus lifted Mary Magdalene
And Mary came with alabaster cruse,
A deed was wrought—but more; that there
was seen
The bond of holy love of which I muse.
Give me, O God, the understanding heart,
Lit with the quickening flame Thou does
impart.

In witnessing Christ's conquest over death, Mary Magdalene spoke to him and he spoke to her. No woman played a more majestic role in Christ's last days. People like Mary Magdalene aid Christianity's survival in perilous times. They also improve the quality of Christian life for themselves and others. Their legacy to the Christian way of life is of far greater value than they or anyone realizes, for their faith is based on reality. Men and women today need to continue to take real leadership in the growth of Christian thought. Intellectual emancipation, if used wisely, can help usher in one of the noblest eras in the history of the Christian faith.

Chapter 49

On Kindness:
Dorcas

(Acts 9:36, 39)

"If a brother or sister is ill-clad and in lack of daily food, and one of you says to them, 'Go in peace, be warmed and filled,' without giving them the things needed for the body, what does it profit? So faith, by itself, if it has not works, is dead" (James 2:15-17).

In the early New Testament church a woman named Dorcas not only gave of herself to others but in her daily life was an example to all believers that miracles abound among practicing Christians, even when it appears that both good works and miracles go unrecognized. When Dorcas was raised from the dead by Peter, those to whom she had given so much, crowded around her. Among these were concerned widows, wearing coats and garments she had made for them. They were ecstatic when they saw her arise and walk forth well and whole again.

What she had shared with them had so realistically met their daily needs that they loved her devotedly. And when she was resurrected from the dead, they were so filled with wonder that they and many others "believed in the Lord."

In Dorcas we see two important patterns for daily living, giving and believing. Too often each is pushed aside for a lesser accomplishment—a limited social success, a wealthy marriage, or a high office in a mediocre organization. Yet the example of Dorcas has survived the centuries. Her endeavors apply to men and women of every age. No doubt she had moments when she thought her life and example had little meaning beyond a few small kindnesses. But after almost two thousand years, Dorcas continues to inspire us with a knowledge of what real service and unselfish giving can mean. If we give of what we have, whether it be money or service or kind words, our lives reach into the infinite, and we suddenly discover God in all his mystery.

Such giving also makes us more conscious of what Kahlil Gibran meant in the first three lines of his essay "On Giving." *The Prophet,* by Kahlil Gibran (1883-1931).

> You give but little when you give of your possessions.
> It is when you give of yourself that you truly give.
> For what are your possessions but things you keep and
>   guard for fear you may need them tomorrow?

Dorcas did not wait until tomorrow to give to others. Each day she served the needy with all she had. She served them with hands that stitched deftly, with a caring spirit that understood their needs, and with a warmth of understanding that drew others to her in a bond of love.

As we learn to serve others, we are taken beyond our own small selves. We begin to see God moving through our lives in wondrous ways, enriching our concept of his universe. Suddenly the selfish pursuits that once shut us in vanish as if they never existed. We learn to believe in wonders, even when outer circumstances may not justify that belief. As we believe in a power beyond ourselves, we draw closer to the marvelous presence of God, "who . . . calls into existence the things that do not exist" (Rom. 4:17), a realization of hope at its best.

Chapter 50

A Wise Participant:
Damaris

(Acts 17:34)

Damaris, one of the devout women of "high standing" in Athens, a city full of idols, is remembered because she applied her heart to wisdom. She belonged to a group sought by Paul while he preached in Athens.

For three weeks he "argued" with the people from the Scriptures, "explaining and proving that it was necessary for the Christ to suffer and to rise from the dead. This Jesus, whom I proclaim to you, is the Christ" (Acts 17:3). Some of the disbelievers called Paul "a babbler," but Damaris listened, understood, and believed his message.

Damaris is probably singled out because in Athens there were so few among the idol worshipers who believed that Paul could establish a church there. The Athenians were made up of two groups, the Epicureans to whom the supreme good in life was personal pleasure, and the Stoics, whose philosophy was one of indifference to either pain or pleasure. Damaris was willing to depart from these commonly accepted beliefs. She listened intently to Paul as he stood in the middle of the Areopagus: "The God who made the world and everything in it does not live in shrines made by man. He gives to all men life and breath. It is in him (Christ) that we live and move and have our being; for we are indeed his offspring.

"Being then God's offspring, we ought not to think that the Diety is like gold, or silver, or stone" (Acts 17:29). Paul then called upon those who worshiped idols to repent if they wanted to be regenerated.

A woman like Damaris had an influence upon unbelievers because she walked where few had dared to go. She had stood against "some of the wicked fellows of the rabble" who had set up such an uproar in the city that the authorities feared an uprising.

It takes much courage and wisdom to be like Damaris; keen intelligence is also needed to think through issues and to go against the popular majority. In Athens Damaris assumed real leadership in the growth of Christian thought. She acted as she thought best, regardless of the power of her adversaries.

The same kind of wisdom is needed today, for new issues, many controversial, arise, and only a few have the courage to take a stand. Damaris did exactly what Jesus would have us do when he said, "Walk while you have the light, lest the darkness overtake you; he who walks in the darkness does not know where he goes. While you have the light, believe in the light, that you may become sons [children] of light" (John 12:35-36).

Jesus also said, "Take my yoke upon you, and learn from me, . . . For my yoke is easy, and my burden is light" (Matt. 11:29-30).

Dr. Elton Trueblood, one of the great spiritual leaders of our time, an author, and the founder of Yokefellows International, reminds us that these words of Christ are applied to all Christians. He further comments,

> So important were women in the infant churches, that we are driven to the conclusion that, without their assistance, survival would not have occurred. In the Church at Philippi, the first on the continent of Europe, it seems evident that the majority were women. In any case, one woman, Lydia, was the first member, and others are mentioned in the eloquent Letter which the Apostle Paul wrote to this little group. When the term "Yokefellow," an apparent synonym for a practising Christian, is employed by the author, he actually gives the name of some of the women members. These were Euodia and Syntyche. The words which mean a great deal to many readers of this Letter, words which have given meaning to Christian discipleship, are as follows, "I ask you also, true Yokefellow, help these women for they have labored side by side with me in the gospel" (Phil. 4:3). When we take these words seriously, as we do, we cannot suppose that the earliest Christian women were mere observers; they were involved in the glorious enterprise as teammates. The words of

Christ, "Take my yoke upon you," applied to all Christians, irrespective of sex. The word "Yokefellow" has no gender.

Women were in the total ministry, because all were needed. Otherwise survival was not possible." (Quarterly Yoke Letter, June 1976).

Chapter 51

A Cradle of Faith:
Home of Eunice and Lois

(2 Tim. 1:5–6)

Timothy, "fellow-laborer in the gospel" with Paul, was nurtured in a cradle of faith by his mother, Eunice, and his grandmother, Lois. It is no wonder he was converted on Paul's first missionary journey, that he was his secretary and helper on his second missionary journey, and that he was accepted as Paul's son. His mother and grandmother had prepared him in faith, and he gave that faith back to Paul when the great apostle most needed him, for Paul's cares were many. He had been deserted by friends and followers; so he was lonely in the human sense, and he loved the young Timothy like a father.

Timothy's mother and grandmother are thought to have been widows, though the Bible does not state that they were. They gave all their time, and thought, love, and prayer to him. Paul never failed to give them credit for Timothy's training.

"I am reminded of your sincere faith, a faith that dwelt first in your grandmother Lois and your mother Eunice and now, I am sure, dwells in you. Hence I remind you to rekindle this gift of God that is within you . . . a spirit of power and love and self-control (2 Tim. 1:5-7).

The spiritually perceptive Paul knew better than any one that faith is a gift from God but that it must be nurtured by loved ones at home. Paul went one step farther. He continued to prepare Timothy spiritually, and he honored him by calling him "My dearly beloved son." Paul became a real father to Timothy, about whose own father and grandfather nothing is known, and like a father, Paul taught Timothy not to wander away from the faith. "But as for you, man of God, shun temptation. Aim at righteousness, godliness, faith, love, steadfastness, gentleness" (1 Tim. 6:11).

These qualities were born in Timothy as an inheritance from Eunice and Lois; yet their nurture and example of faith were ever like a light around their promising child. In upholding faith, love, and hope in their son, they later helped him to face life gloriously and valiantly in the almost daily presence of Paul.

The faith Timothy received early was like the grain of mustard seed about which Christ spoke. Like Jesus, Timothy learned early that nothing was impossible. His faith grew until it was like the faith evidenced by works about which James spoke.

"What does it profit . . . if a man says he has faith but has not works? Can his faith save him? If a brother and sister is ill-clad and in lack of daily food, and one of you says to them, 'Go in peace, be warmed and filled,' without giving them the things needed for the body, what does it profit? So faith by itself, if it has no works, is dead. . . . Was not Abraham our father justified by works, when he offered his son Isaac upon the altar? You see that faith was active along with his works, and faith was completed by works, . . . You see that a man is justified by works and not by faith alone" (James 2:14-17, 21-22, 24).

Timothy also possessed the true wisdom about which James asked, "Who is wise and understanding among you? By his good life let him show his works in the meekness of wisdom. But if you have bitter jealousy and selfish ambition in your hearts, do not boast and be false to the truth. This wisdom is not such as comes down from above, but is earthly, unspiritual, devilish. . . . But the wisdom from above is first pure, then peaceable, gentle, open to reason, full of mercy and good fruits, without uncertainty or insincerity" (James 3:13-15, 17).

Chapter 52

Light in God's Word:
Priscilla

(Acts 18:2, 18, 28; Rom. 16:3; 1 Cor. 16:19; 2 Tim. 4:19)

The best-known woman teacher in the New Testament church, Priscilla had a penetrating and profound insight into God's Word as brought to her by Paul. In his deep understanding of the crucifixion and resurrection, Paul gave new dimension to the master's teachings. Priscilla was one of Paul's most competent and inspired pupils. She took up Christ's cross and went forth to expound messianic hopes more accurately to Apollos, a Jew from Alexandria, described as "an eloquent man, well versed in the scriptures" (Acts 18:24).

Not only was Priscilla blessed to have Paul as her teacher but also to have the cooperation of her husband, Aquila. Together she and Aquila "expounded the word of God more accurately" when they went to Ephesus, where they first met Apollos, who is credited with founding the church at Corinth. Through Priscilla and Aquila, Apollos learned the spiritual meaning of baptism through the Holy Spirit, not fully understood in the early ministry of John the Baptist. Although Priscilla and Aquila walked side by side in all they did, Priscilla was probably the more profound teacher of the two.

"In the beginning was the Word, and the Word was with God, and the Word was God. . . . all things were made through him, and without him was not anything made . . . In him was life, and the life was the light of men" (John 1:1-4). Committed Christians like Priscilla render a great service to the Church when they devote themselves to teaching the Word of God. They set an example of how to walk in his transcendent power. Learning and teaching the Bible is the direct result of study, sacrifice, suffering, and dedication. Light then comes into the Word, and one teacher passes it on to another, who like Apollos may search but not always understand without skilled and inspiring instruction.

Today's teachers in the church and Sunday school, as well as ministers and evangelists, soon learn that they must be "united in the same mind and the same judgment," or the gospel loses its meaning and power for newborn Christians, who may pick up false knowledge. In the minds of the humble and the sincere, teachers like Priscilla gain a new spiritual awareness that must be cherished and shared. Teachers of the gospel soon discover they must seek to live in the light if they are to cast a lasting light upon others.

Vast storehouses of knowledge now await teachers of the Word. Gigantic leaps have been made into the past and the future through the explosion in knowledge, through worldwide, mass communications, including dial telephones in which one may speak through the void of space into all parts of the world. Add to these the magic of printing, radio and television and the power of cathedrals, churches and synagogues all over the world, and one finds the words of the Bible ring out loudly and clearly, unlike that at any time in history.

We are living in the golden age of Bible translation. Expositors of the Bible have at their command more important new translations than at any other period in history. There was a time, beginning in the early fifth century and extending to the Reformation of Western Christendom between the fourteenth and seventeenth centuries, that scholars had little but St. Jerome's Latin Version of the Bible, most frequently referred to as the Vulgate, finished in AD 404.

In these first centuries it was impossible to circulate the Bible widely. It was not until 1611 that the King James Version, commonly known in England as the Authorized Version, was published. But in the last few decades important new translations have been published, including the Revised Standard Version, the New English Bible with the Apocrypha, and the New American Bible, the first important Catholic Bible since the Douay-Rheims (1582-1609) version. This last was compiled largely by Catholic scholars, assisted by "separated brothers" so that "all

Christians may be able to use the Bible." Other new editions are the Jerusalem Bible, translated from the French by Dominican scholars in Jerusalem, and the New American Standard, the most literal of modern translations. The new translations of the American Bible Society is called Good News for Modern Man, and another new translation is the Living Bible. Only the first five books of the new Jewish Bible have been completed.

The miracle of all of these translations is that the Bible, the greatest of all books, was first compiled in tiny Canaan, called in turn Palestine, the Holy Land and Israel. This small area, no larger than the state of Indiana, gave to the world a book that permanently changed the course of history.

Like the monks of old, expositors today work on through heartache, disappointment, illness, sorrow, interruption, and outside responsibilities; yet interpretation of the Bible continues. The successful dissemination of the Bible is due in large measure to the work of dedicated scholars, teachers, and ministers in every part of the world. They make it come alive to millions, even the ignorant and disinterested, who may later take up the Word of God and carry it forward.

Seekers of Bible truths still walk the way of the cross and discover there is always room at the cross. Even as they pass on their heritage amid much suffering, others come to know a God who loves them, heals them, and sets them on new paths. Priscilla lives on as one of the wisest and most knowledgable women of the early church. She was active in small groups at Ephesus, Corinth, and Rome and taught in her own Church of the Household at both Ephesus and Corinth. A church was named for her on the Aventine Hill in Rome. Priscilla probably had few handwritten scrolls, if any, to work with; yet she possessed so much, including a close friendship with Paul, through whom she gained a deeper understanding of Christ himself.

Epilogue

Certain of these women reveal that we have but to seek wisdom from God, and it comes with the promise of his security. Some Bible women built their lives around that which is good; others chose foolish ways. Each has influenced civilization in one way or another, for good or for evil. Wisdom was born with creation, but it has taken men and women centuries to learn its secrets, to fathom its meaning, and to discover that wisdom and understanding walk side by side. The living God is all about us; we need but to seek his presence. He does not fail us.

"So teach us to number our days, that we may apply our
hearts unto wisdom.
Return, O Lord, how long? and let it repent thee concerning
thy servants.
O satisfy us early with thy mercy;
that we may rejoice and be glad in all our days.
Make us glad according to the days wherein thou has afflicted
us, and the years wherein we have seen evil.
Let thy work appear to thy servants, and thy glory unto
their children.
And let the beauty of the Lord our God be upon us: and
establish thou the work of our hands upon us; yea, the work
of our hands establish thou it."

Ps. 90:12–17, KJV